THAT WAS THEN,
This Is Now

FINDING HEALING THROUGH CONNECTION, REFLECTION, & SELF-CARE

by Rosemary Dunn Dalton LCSW

*Thank you to my friend, editor, and
sister writer, Melissa Michaels*

ROSEMARY DUNN DALTON'S PREVIOUS BOOKS

Lesbian Psychologies, Coeditor (University of Illinois Press, 1987)

Lamenting Lost Fathers: Adult Daughters Search for the Message of the Father (iUniverse, 2004)

Arches Treasure & Mystery at the Escalantes (iUniverse, 2008)

Bandon-Vernal Transgender Mystery & The Jacksonville-Donner Story (iUniverse, 2013)

Lost and Found (local printing, 2015)

Edited, typeset, and designed by
Michaels & Michaels Creative, LLC

First printing, 2015

ISBN 978-0-692-53936-1

Table of Contents

You have to be hard on yourself, be honest, and look yourself in the face. You have to get rid of the surplus, the hatred, and the excessive love.

—SUZANNE VALADON, ARTIST, PARIS

CHAPTER I

Personal History as a Predictor

UNDERSTANDING THE ORIGIN of our attitudes, strengths, and vulnerabilities involves going inside and asking important questions. This doesn't mean we mirror our parents and ancestors; it means our reactive emotional and physical systems live in an environment that stimulated rational and irrational responses, defenses, and ways of viewing the world. Going inside may mean envisioning the bedroom where we slept as a child and remembering the ceiling, the pictures on the walls, the doorway, the windows. What grew or laid outside the windows may have offered an emotional escape from the everydayness of our lives. The bedroom was the intimate place where we rested, left others behind, and felt our aloneness, even if we shared a room with siblings or parents.

I shared a bedroom with my father until I was around six. He had a regular-sized bed that seemed much smaller than those I see today. I was in a nearby crib. I don't have a strong visual memory of that time, but I imagine I heard his breathing, which was probably soothing for me.

I was later transferred to a different room with a wrought-iron bed, which I shared with my two sisters, one four years older and the other eleven years my senior. That room firmly resides in my mind. I slept in the middle, squashed and jostled about. I was the youngest of eight children, with twenty-four years separating the eldest and me. I was a cuddling type, which prevails today as I snuggle with my partner.

Where did you live when you were young? Which house sticks in your mind the most—the one you might refer to as "home"? Who was there with you? What do you recall about them and their most prevalent characteristics—physical and emotional?

I remember my mother's housedresses, as she called them. Repeatedly repaired, the front was tattered from leaning over the washing machine and manipulating a roller that squeezed water from the clothes. One time when she was a few weeks pregnant, she caught her hair in the ringer and aborted a fetus. This is a scary thought as I examine my mother's perils, strengths, and ability to sustain emotional injury.

My mother had ten pregnancies, one being a miscarriage and another born dead. The stillborn deeply affected my brothers and sisters. No doubt this is one of the reasons my mother eventually sequestered herself in her own bedroom, relegating me, as the youngest, to the back room—with my father.

Just before my twelfth birthday, my mother arranged for me to join my father on a train trip from our hometown of Detroit, Michigan, to California, where my two elder sisters lived with their husbands and children. Not yet a teenager, I was an aunt to thirteen grandchildren. During this visit, I slept in the same bed with my father. I had just started piecing together thoughts about sex, and I asked my sister if I could get pregnant by sleeping with my dad. She laughed and explained sexual intercourse to me, although I wouldn't have phrased it that way then. When we returned, I met with my best friend, and she, too, had just learned about these things. We laughed and laughed and said no way were we going to do anything like that!

What have I uncovered by these incidents? I can understand now why I felt closest to my father, why I understood and accepted him more than I did my mother. I learned I can be close to another person, cuddle, and show my affection without being concerned about sexual overtones. I felt safe with the primary man in my life. I have always been close to girlfriends and women friends. As the youngest of eight, I spent a lot of time alone and invented ways to seek connection with others, perhaps to thwart loneliness.

Connection

MY FATHER USED to tease me and say, "Watch out, or I'll cuff your ear!" This always made me laugh. Now I picture this man of white hair and round body posing a teasing threat to me, and I realize it was then that I stopped being fearful of reprisal from him or taking him seriously. This helps today as I examine my relationships with boys and men. I find that in spite of the everyday threat of violence against women, I tend to be trusting and helpful. I understand much of what makes men the way they are, what they are up against in a culture that aggrandizes and then deflates them with phrases like, "You know how men are."

Women generally seek connection with men, often expecting them to act like women. At least this is my impression, and I generalize in this way to make a point. Culturally and ethnically, men are impacted by society in different ways than women. These differences make relationships challenging but also potentially fulfilling because of the contrasts. Clones are boring. Living with a reflection of ourselves can lead to apathy.

Exploring questions about our parents can be illuminating. Who were they? What did you witness in their relationship? How were respect and diverse opinions integrated into their daily lives? What did you learn? What about you do you associate with the qualities of your parents? So often we hear remarks like, "You look just like her" and "You remind me of your mother." These words are sometimes uttered as a compliment but more often as a form of blackmail. How do you feel about these comments?

I never wanted to be like my mother. She was tired and worn by the time I was born, and she always reminded me she was old enough to be my grandmother. She looked like my grandmother, with her grey hair and stocky body. Sometimes I was embarrassed by this fact. But I still wanted to be close to her, to be understood by her. I wanted her to want to be with me, but this did not happen until I was into my twenties—a bit late for me to learn to respect and value her opinions. Now her words ring in my ears, and I often quote her. As an older woman, I value her health-related warnings, her stressing that rest cures all, her ability to free herself from the tirades and PLAY! She danced, ice-skated, played cards with her women friends. She enjoyed herself. What a wonderful message for me now that I am an elder.

My mother was close to her children in different ways; each was acknowledged for their strengths, as limited as her vision was for them. In the context of her era, she did pretty well, although I never appreciated her perspective. She idealized my oldest brother and at times put him before her relationship with my father. I watched this bone of contention play out throughout my life. What did I learn from this? I saw she wanted connection and would try to understand her family, often only within the limits of what served her. She was an aging woman of great faith. She prayed all pain away. This I did not appreciate, but now I understand it worked for her. I'm trying in my own way to emulate that practice. Her version of spirituality serves as a model as I seek my own, though different from hers.

How do you define connection/disconnection? Psychology tells us humans are wired to seek connection. Some say disconnection is the root of all disturbances, injuries, and violence.

In what ways do you practice connection? Have you carved out your own path to friendships? Do you reach out? Are you the one who initiates, or do you wait for others to do so? Are you resentful when they don't, or do you take the step toward them anyway? As people grow older, isolation can set in, with more rules for and less patience with others. How do you address this? Are you paving the way for your future by nurturing old and new relationships? What did your family teach you about connection? Do you stay connected to them, even if they falter? Do you keep the memory of them although you may have grown apart?

When I was in the seventh and eighth grades, my parents took extended trips, thinking my sister, four years my senior, and I were old enough to handle their absence. I spent a good deal of time alone while she sought out her friends. I purposely set times at our house for pajama parties or for a friend to spend the night. I knew then connection was essential to stemming loneliness. I associate those early days in my father's and siblings' bedrooms with my limited ability to be alone for periods of time. I am a busy woman, just like my mother was.

My mother was close to her mother. Every Saturday, they went "downtown" shopping. My grandmother would buy her a dress. Mom was not the kind of person who expected this generosity and was surprised to find her mother so giving. Gram always gave money to my mother, who could not otherwise have afforded life with so many children. In turn, my mother gave me money when I was raising my family. Now, when I give money to others, I give it with the agreement that I do not wish to be repaid. This replays my agreements with my mother. She always knew I would be unable to repay the money she "loaned" me, even though the sums were modest— except when she ended up with my car payments when I was nineteen.

Disconnection

FOR DECADES, THE discussion regarding the affects of drugs and alcohol has been impacting the way psycho-therapy is approached. All mental health clinics conduct a drug and alcohol assessment as part of their evaluation.

It has been over twenty years since I stopped drinking. While raising my family, I monitored my drinking to match our situation. This meant drinking in the evenings and not to excess. We also smoked pot together when they were older. I look back at those times and remember them as happy, filled with fun experiences and laughter. We were a tightknit family, and our closeness was pur-poseful and meaningful. My children were adults when I stopped drinking. It was then that I felt the disconnec-tion. We hung out together until the partying got too intense and was no longer enjoyable, at which point I left. I feel sad because I thought my children would follow my lead. This eventually held true for my daughter, but not my son.

In reviewing our times together, I am grateful we stayed close as a family and as confidents, too. I wonder if the disconnections would have happened sooner if I had not also been part of "the party." When my children reached their twenties and thirties, there was repair work necessary as they each faced life's challenges.

As a psychotherapist, when I sit with a couple and one is using substances and the other is trying to connect, often there is a realization that they must face the loss of what I call the user's "best friend." Is this friend a stand-in for the partner—is it there that the user feels connection? Is this a missing factor in their relationship? Will he or she give up the use of drugs and alcohol to be more present in the relationship? If so, how will they withdraw and move closer? Rehabilitation may or may not be a choice. Rehabilitation programs help the addict dig deeper into the early messages of childhood as well investigating relational patterns involving substance abuse. This is helpful. Alcoholics Anonymous provides a daily check-in to help the person stay sober. These steps help repair disconnection.

A woman speaks of the loss of her father at age ten and her mother's inability to adjust to his death. It became the daughter's burden to walk their mother through this terrible loss. The devastation never lifted, however, and in her thirties, she is still holding her mother's emotional life. She longs for connection but is coming to terms with the reality that her mother does not want that kind of relationship with her. This is painful, and the woman must now examine how this has impacted her own intimate relationships and how much she continues this caretaking role with her respective partners. The work of uncovering the rage connected with the loss of her childhood can begin when she is ready to examine her relationship with her mother. Unfortunately, the cultural message of "she did the best she could" is a barrier against the wretched realization that she cannot have the mother she wants. Through counseling, she can review the circumstances of her early life, face the losses, and give up longing for the good mother. The choices mothers make in parenting can eventually be understood only after women look at what really happened and replace the mother-longing with self-loving. Eventually, she will be able to see her mother in the context of the era of her mother's early life and the consequences that got played out in her mother's role as parent.

As the youngest child, I was often in the care of my next-in-line sister. She didn't like this situation unless it served her. Typical of sibling behavior, she would play with me when she had no alternative. We fought a lot, and I knew she resented me. In time, she sought solace away from our family and pretty much became a missing person. We didn't become "close" until she met her husband-to-be. He loved to chat about politics, history, and his life experiences, and I was his pupil.

We had great times together as he, my sister, and I raised our families—until their marriage began to fall apart. He axed me from the triangle, and eventually, my sister told me she wanted no contact as she tried to hang onto her marriage. This hurt, mostly because I felt sympathy for her and the futility of her resolve. Two years after their separation, she showed up and apologized. We managed to recoup some of our relationship for a while. When I stopped drinking, however, our communication changed. How do you repair a long-term relationship when there has been this kind of breach? It took me two decades to realize the severance of our connection stems not only from her taking a "break" from me but also from earlier childhood disconnections. No matter how I try to frame those times as then versus now, in my own personal work, mistrust prevails.

Forgiveness is a wonderful concept and can be deeply felt, but it is different from acceptance of the events that made us who we are today. Acceptance involves facing the realities we bury so as to continue each day. Forgiveness is a spiritual experience and involves forgiving ourselves—for the obsessions, the misgivings, the ways in which we diluted ourselves. This is the work of counseling.

Acceptance

MY MIDDLE DAUGHTER, Molly, is multiply-disabled and brain-injured. This occurred at birth; within nine months, she was diagnosed as "hopelessly retarded." That was the language of the day. Starting when Molly was two and a half and continuing to age four, we conducted a rehabilitation program from our home. This involved my working with her on the floor most of the day and coordinating exercises with volunteers on a "patterning" table four times a day. I, too, grew during this time, and my political and social consciousness radically changed. I understood I was now a minority and committed myself to social change. This personal transformation created a schism between my husband and me. Within a few years, a major disconnection became apparent, compounded by the impact of my husband's alcoholism on me. We then divorced—the ultimate disconnection.

Ethical Disconnection

WORK DISSATISFACTION MAY involve turning our heads when ethical problems exist, causing a serious disconnect. Systems may feel beyond our control, whether we are working at an automobile plant, used car lot, academic setting, federal agency, or county services. Voicing our objections may cause termination.

How do we reconcile our personal moral code with perceived ethical violations? How do we surface without being labeled a whistleblower? How can we stay within the bounds of our responsibilities and stay out of trouble? When this dilemma creates physical and emotional problems, it is time to solve the problem. How do you do that? In my view, suffering physical manifestations that are job-related may be a bottom line. Sometimes spirituality can buoy a person through the conflict. One woman closes her door at the beginning of each day and practices a centering meditation along with a prayer. This is intentional living for her as it carries her through the day. When she becomes overly anxious, she concentrates on the ceiling as a grounding exercise to help clear her thoughts.

Living in an emotionally or physically abusive relationship involves daily disconnection, which wears down the victim. Battering takes its toll as self-esteem plummets; eventually, the sufferer may feel worthless. The public cry of "Why doesn't she just leave?" does not help. The answer is almost immaterial; whether she leaves or stays, she needs financial and emotional support.

Joan tells of how her husband tracked everything in her life, even though she worked and was the main financial contributor to their lives. He made sure she had no money, packed her lunch, prohibited a cell phone, told her what she could wear, and kept her from seeing her friends. He was the main caretaker for their son, three years old. She tried to leave several times, but each time, he convinced her to stay by threatening suicide. She needed an advocate and a plan, but first, she needed to believe she could make the break and keep her child. His gun collection added to her fear. In time, after extensive convincing and maneuvering, she was able to collect her son, under police protection, and retreat to Dunn House, a shelter for battered women and their children.

In 1977, our women's center sponsored a workshop on Household Violence, and the issue surfaced for the first time in a public way. Many of us were caught off-guard as woman after woman came forward, taking all the risks that accompany exposing their husbands and families to the reality that they were under threat in their own homes. Educating the public, mental health professionals, police, and social service agencies was a daunting task. Within a year after we initiated the Jackson County Task Force on Household Violence, my personal experience as a survivor of domestic abuse surfaced for me.

Over the next few years, we set up shelters in friends' homes, then in rentals, and later in a consistent home environment. Today, this program is thriving. Women may leave a violent situation up to seven to ten times before they are able to get free. The success of this service is reinforced by the criminal justice system raising police awareness. In addition, domestic and sexual violence prevention programs continue to offer training for volunteers and agency staff.

The Larger Picture

THE EVENING NEWS can create extreme unrest, worry, and disconnection from the larger world. Focusing on the suffering of people who live with fear and learning of items like the drones' destruction of villages and lives can be debilitating. Some of us pray, some write their legislators and Congress, others engage in public protests and demonstrations. Many of us have difficulty reconciling the cognitive dissonance of living in a country that espouses freedom while freedoms are being curtailed, nationally and internationally. We ask: What are we to do? What is enough? Surrendering to a democratic process while it justifies war and violence has caused people to stop voting and drop out of political discussions and concerns. Focusing on the quality of our daily lives and helping others is what we *can* do. It may seem unrelated, but it contributes to the larger quality of community life. We live with the realities of poverty and hopelessness within the boundaries of our urban and suburban lives, which makes our hearts heavy. For me, there is happiness through appreciation for birds, animals, and other species that tell us life goes on. I find solace and fun in writing mystery stories, which enables me to "rest" from the stress of living with stories of struggle in my counseling practice.

Clinical diagnosis can create disconnection and misunderstanding. Transgender individuals face fear of the lack of acceptance as they find their personal path of transition. Traditionally, longing to be of another sex was viewed as pathological and labeled gender identity disorder/gender dysphoria. This situation is doubly painful when parents, partners, or children do not support efforts to address the dilemma for the transgender person. Support can be pursued in the community, which helps, while counseling can address preconceived notions. Often the person goes to a pastor or minister, who may not understand the underlying despair. When I set up a small committee of therapists who wanted to be educated, a generous female-affirmed "trans" shared her experiences with them. She described her genital reconstruction, breast implants, and daily hormonal treatments and expressed profound happiness with her decision.

As a witness, I am guided and educated by the trans community. I can spend time on the phone directing the person to a support group and online connections as well as clearing up the idea that he or she is mentally ill. This may mean constructing language to ease communication with parents, releasing them from the tyrannical power parents or religious persons may wield over them.

Questions to Think About

1. What is your understanding of connection/disconnection?

2. In what ways do you seek connection?

3. Have you carved out your own path to friendships?

4. Do you reach out?

5. Are you the initiator in friendships, or do you wait for others to do so?

6. When they don't initiate, are you resentful, or do you step toward them anyway?

7. As people grow older, isolation can set in, with more rules for others and less patience. How do you address this?

8. Are you paving the way for your future by nurturing old and new relationships?

9. What did your family teach you about connection?

10. Do you stay connected with them even if they falter?

11. Do you nurture the memory of them although you may have grown apart?

If you have a body in which you are born to a certain amount of pain ... why should you not, when the occasion presents, draw from this same body the maximum of pleasure?

—ISADORA DUNCAN, *My Life*

CHAPTER II

Denial and Other Defenses

A MAN IS living with his wife, who has been diagnosed with Alzheimer's disease. Serving as her caretaker, he refuses to accept outside help. He says she doesn't want that. She has stopped reading and roams about the house aimlessly, yet she dresses herself every day. She enjoys television and sometimes tackles a crossword puzzle or a game of Scrabble with the help of her husband. He is distressed at times but not all the time. He remains hopeful and enjoys his wife. She is about to turn ninety; he is eighty, in good shape for his age. Many of their friends have died, and he is isolating more each day. We talk of small ways in which he can integrate a friend or two or talk to a neighbor. He is puzzled as to why his neighbors no longer make eye contact or drop by. I explain that, given their ages, they are likely undergoing similar problems and may be emotionally unable to reach out. I encourage him to be the one to reach out, to make just one phone call a week, to continue going to the gym. Most of all, I encourage him to figure out a way to have someone relieve him of his duties. This takes a while. It is hard for him to give up control. All of this is completely understandable. Eventually, we uncover that there is an old friend his wife trusts. He decides to ask this friend to visit weekly so he can leave for short periods.

This gentleman could easily be characterized as being in *denial*. People are attached to the use of this term when judging others for not doing what they think should happen. It may be true, however, that he uses denial to avoid facing the inevitable loss of his wife as her mind diminishes and she progresses to her eventual demise.

This defense works well for the time being as he makes attempts to take better care of himself, physically and emotionally. He must stay in his daily life without giving in to fear of the future.

When my disabled daughter was diagnosed, a friend said I was in denial. Maybe she was correct in that I did not get out my crystal ball and predict how my life would be affected by keeping her in our family setting rather than placing her in an institution, which my friends had expected.

Denial is a catch-all term for a complex defense mechanism. Defenses are life-saving and help us navigate the world; it is best not to give them up until we can replace them with other defenses. For example, when my gentleman client does have to make decisions about a different care plan, perhaps out of the home, he will need to replace denial with another defense, like believing things will get better. This will work fine as he goes through his own adjustment to living alone. He speaks of moving to a different climate, but he probably won't do that, even though he has family there. He thinks he will be too afraid. No doubt a social worker would recommend he stay put; I will walk him through his ambivalence and help him regulate his fear. He believes it is never too late, and so do I. Maybe that's denial!

Projection

Projection IS COMMONLY used in discussions as people try to understand why they are misunderstood in relationships. We all use projection as a defense. To justify our perceptions, we project onto others what we want to see. Sometimes it helps to make the other person the bad guy if we cannot face up to our accountability in situations. Often, we unconsciously judge another by the way they talk or what region or country they are from. Classism permeates our culture; our economic and social systems depend on it. Those of us who have been fortunate enough to get degrees can easily delude ourselves into thinking we are middle class or beyond. Yet in reality we have no concept of money, real money—the money that runs the world, that pays for projects through lobbyists and corporate connections. The average person cannot keep track of political systems and how they connect with wealth. This is a form of self-deception or perhaps denial, which is necessary as we face our daily lives.

American culture promotes the notion that everyday people can strike it rich through television contests, the lottery, and fast money-making ventures. This is tempting as an escape from our worries and the consistently increasing costs of living, maintaining health, and raising families. One man drives his partner crazy with each passing idea of how to get rich. This is his addiction, and he cannot set himself free when an idea comes up or something promises great wealth. This creates a disconnection in their relationship with the constant temptation to bail him out when he goes too far with these "investments." He suffers under the illusion that money or material resources will solve his problems; his partner is the opposite in that she conserves. She is a Boston CEO and saves for the future for their family of four. This places tremendous stress on their relationship, and, with help, they manage to keep communicating and try to be separate yet supportive in their differences. This idea that opposites attract is true in this case; they have the opportunity to transform themselves and fight the projection that could easily permeate their relationship. Consistent acknowledgment of the fear that underlies the issues is challenging but possible.

In my traditional social work training, I resist viewing people as emotionally "sick." Mental illness is real and diagnosis can be helpful, but underneath the labels we can find a way to measure people's response to their environment. Given enough emotional, physical, and psychological pressure, all of us are vulnerable to "outbreaks" of personality features and mood disorders. In addition, medical interventions with psychotropic drugs continue to be life-saving. The Wellesley Center for Women has framed defenses as "strategies of disconnection," which moves us away from pathological contexts to the normalization of defenses.

A number of years ago, I was surprised with a subpoena I felt was unjustly served. I had never been sued before, and in the end, a settlement was reached that confirmed the individual wanted to punish me for a statement I had made in a meeting. This taught me to temper my natural inclination toward righteous indignation and be more careful as a social work provider. I paid a heavy price, however, because the stress response I had at that moment of serving profoundly impacted my life. Every defense I had rushed to my aid as my body shuddered with fear. I knew I was experiencing symptoms of PTSD and that they would continue for years. Friends helped me through this event as did my insurance provider, but within six months, I lost every hair on my body. Diagnosed with alopecia areata, I will never again grow hair on my head. They say hair is a woman's crowning glory, which now makes me laugh as I have replaced the baldness with art. Everywhere I go, people stop to view my tattoos and show me their own. I feel fortunate to have access to a segment of the community I may never have known. I use denial to move through the prejudice society has about tattoos. There is a loosening of this projection as tattooing transcends class divides, but only to a certain degree. One day, I am seen as a rebel, another day an innovator, the next day a nutcase. Most of the time, I am viewed as a cancer survivor, and this engenders a kinder sort of projection. People either identify with me, sympathize, or feel grateful that whatever I have has escaped them!

Projective Identification

CLINICAL ASSESSMENT CAN be perceived as harsh but is also helpful; it provides a handle, a way of looking at behaviors and is necessary for insurance reimbursements. Most working people want to use their health insurance to help pay for counseling. As a feminist therapist, I long resisted labels, but I have learned how to use diagnosis as a tool in teaching students and clients. *Projective identification* is considered a serious defense or a way of dodging emotions in a relationship. This complex defense is difficult to explain. In one couple, a double bind kept showing up in counseling. They often mirrored each other in their responses, and it was difficult to sort out how each honestly felt. Barbara was frequently furious with her partner, Susan, denying statements Barbara said she had made, acting in ways Barbara could not recall or admit to. With projective identification, the person may feel things that surprise her or she does not identify with. A simple explanation is that one partner projects onto the other her feelings, and the partner expresses those feelings. Sometimes people say they don't know how they landed in a situation or how something happened. Psychologists may view this as one person projecting onto the other her dark side or darker feelings. If there is enough anger and dysfunction in a relationship, this may be the case. Maybe it is too late for counseling, then. This is the type of relationship found between many parents and adult children. It is sad, but in my work, it is helpful to explain this defense to couples so they can identify when they are resentful and judging their partners. Each has the responsibility to develop ways of communicating that enable them to reach this level of honesty.

Identification with the Aggressor

A FAMOUS PUBLIC example of projective identification is found in Patty Hearst, the daughter of newspaper and media magnate William Randolph Hearst. Much has been written about her because of the images of her as a participant in a bank robbery. Over time, the public labeled Ms. Hearst as having been "brainwashed" or as a victim of the Stockholm syndrome. As her story gradually unraveled, it turned out to be not that simple. She was repeatedly raped and held captive in various ways; eventually, she bonded with a perpetrator who was less threatening than the others. This defense of *identification with the aggressor* ultimately saved her life. We can only imagine what it took to unravel this distortion after her release.

Women who are held captive by their partners and experience this kind of abuse may develop this defense while sorting out the confusion of living with someone who is violent one day and acts lovingly the next. Deciding to let go of the illusion of Mr. Nice Guy to save ourselves is hard work. Clinicians still trying to answer the question "Why does she stay?" can better understand this defense mechanism in the context of studies of the brain during a stress response. Generalizations of gender differences tend to be worn out, but one study concluded women do not necessarily have a flight-or-fight response;

rather, they may have a "tend-and-mend" reaction. It takes courage to admit we are powerless to change another person, especially if he or she is a longtime partner. Biological determinism does not explain why women try to do their best to make a relationship work or parent in certain ways.

Resistance

A HELPFUL DEFENSE when we are not ready to confront personal change, resistance is persistent as an internal tug of war. My partner and I respond differently to demands or situations. I tease her because she tends to wait and contemplate; I tend to strike while the iron is hot. I have learned to look inside to check my level of anxiety when I *have* to get things done. I also have learned to temper my comments or demands as I anticipate how they will be responded to.

My mother had to hold back whatever my father did not want to hear. She was a master of timing. She never brought up topics before my father had dinner or it was too late at night. She acquired these practices after experiencing enough episodes of his raging. Early on, I figured out what she was doing. I think she took the kinder and easier path. I now realize it makes sense to get a reading before bringing up controversial subjects. It reminds me of "hungry, angry, lonely, and tired," a self-examination measure Alcoholics Anonymous recommends. Understanding our significant others', partners', family's, and friends' resistance is key to acceptance. It also helps us give up the need to control or be in control. Maybe this is why people pray: to surrender to powerlessness.

My friend talks of trying to understand her adult children, who are so different from her. She is a tidy, organized person. This helps her stay calm and feel in control. Her daughter and son are the opposite in that they live with "stuff" all over their lives—piles in every room and unfinished projects everywhere. She tries to understand them by facing her own resistance and need to control. Her history as a bank attendant taught her the importance of accuracy and balance. She was an excellent worker because of her early training in her parents' home; they paid attention to her and the details of daily life. She wasn't overtly punished for breaking the rules but instead was subtly shut out of the conversations. She recalls the pain of their shunning and now understands why she is a "neat freak." She calls her children "pack rats." Both terms represent defense systems designed to help them stay calm. Criticism only increases anxiety. This resistance to order can be a way of staying a bit out of control, which actually helps her children feel they have more control.

Working with partners who have different organizational styles can be challenging. The more organized person may be the one to work on giving in to some form of disorder and learning how to manage his or her anxiety through outlets or hobbies that take them away from the disarray. When couples truly care for one another, compromises can be made. One approach involves deciding on places for certain piles and ways to keep most of the counters clear instead of trying to restructure the whole house.

Sometimes couples compare the partner's habits to their parents' ways. This is helpful if it leads to breaking familial patterns. For myself, I look back at my mother's storage in her basement and attic and remember how much fun it was to go through the bags and boxes of clothes, books, dresser scarves, gloves, hats, old letters, and photographs. My mother raised all of her children in the same house, so memories of events and our family's history were easily preserved. I can still smell the musty scents of those cherished items as I revisit the wonderful adventure of going through my mother's things. Through my own family's moves from Midwest to West to East and back to West, many of our items have been saved, but now I ask, for whom? I have no grandchildren, and the progeny stop with my adult children. The way I defend against sadness and disappointment is by writing. What a delightful defense this is! My daughter Brigid is a busy bee like her mother; she may be substituting friendships and work for her lack of a family. She is a creative person, great with people, and loves to connect, so this defense works well for her.

Brigid and I recently viewed Mariel Hemingway's biographical documentary, *Running from Crazy*, a stunning representation of her life as the granddaughter of revered writer Ernest Hemingway. It is an exploration into her family history and the issue of suicide. Her disclosures about her incestuous father and the effects on her sisters seemed downplayed. Brigid had a strong reaction to this film in that it gave her an opportunity to reflect on her life, expressing gratitude for not being a victim of incest. She spoke of her concern that incest was not treated as the cause or result of suicide and mental illness. I sensed Ms. Hemingway at the time of the film was not completely ready to accept that this particular trauma may be viewed as originating from mental illness. She admittedly does not want to totally face the fear and pain of this reality. Denial has served her well so far. Trauma-informed training addresses this strategy, and Judith Herman explores the connection between trauma and denial so powerfully in *Trauma and Recovery*. For many, the deleterious effects of sexual abuse have been surfacing more since the Catholic Church has been confronted with disclosures by victims of sex abuse by priests.

Procrastination

THE PAIN OF indecisiveness, *procrastination* may be connected with the inability to let go of material things. When sitting with someone who cannot make up their mind or who may have positioned themselves in either/ or situations in which both alternatives don't quite feel right, it is tempting to take a firm position and force a decision. This, however, leads to more anxiety and self-criticism. Rather, what is required is walking through each aspect of the situation, breaking it down into smaller parts, and waiting for the moment of realization.

After moving from Detroit to Oregon, I spent every night of the first three months figuring out finances and a way to return. The patience it took to stay put and have faith that things would work out, that I would come to appreciate my surroundings, was overwhelming. In Oregon, my children and I were in school, which soon grounded me, and their trust in me helped me to settle into a new life, 3,000 miles away from my family of origin. Intuitively, I knew rural life in the mountains and a college town was better than living in Detroit as it gradually deteriorated, abandoned by people fleeing to the suburbs. My children thrived in Oregon, even while being challenged by absence of divergent cultures.

Almost ten years later, my daughter Brigid and I moved to Boston the day after she graduated from high school. I had written a book on fathers and daughters and wanted to get published; we both needed to leave small-town life. Parting from my adult son and disabled daughter was a brave thing to do, and I think we both wanted a break from the responsibility. Molly was situated in a group home we had initiated; Tom was twenty-one and said goodbye with great ambivalence. I was able to push through procrastination, thanks to Brigid, who warned she was going with or without me!

The rewarding aspects of moving to Boston were not apparent at first. Within a year, however, I started a private practice, got involved in lesbian and gay politics, and became chair of the Lesbian, Gay, Bisexual Political Alliance, a major political organization. Gay men were dying at a horrible rate, and simultaneously, lesbians were taking the lead in organizations. There was no room for procrastination as I leapt into an arena where I had little experience.

Dissociation

TODAY, WHEN I arrived at my favorite coffee shop, I realized I had "spaced out" all of my usual signposts in my walk. This is a form of *dissociation*, a defense we naturally employ when our mind needs a rest. Generally, this defense is seen as unhealthy and indeed is a state of mind/emotion that blocks out what is happening right before us. Rape survivors report experiencing this state of mind during the assault, perhaps as a life-saving defense. This becomes worrisome if the survivor continues to revisit this state during the course of a normal day or when trying to be intimate. A rekindling of the assault may occur then or at other times when she is triggered. Often a trigger is unpredictable and may turn up in times that don't make sense. It may be a scent, a color, a song, or a situation.

It takes years to become mindful of triggers and protect ourselves from reacting in unhelpful ways. I have trained myself to walk through the feeling/trigger associated with the subpoena episode by becoming aware of my body's responses and practicing several thought-stopping techniques. More importantly, I try to have mercy for myself as the little girl who used to get into trouble with the nuns and other authority figures and acknowledge my need now to be "perfect."

Questions to Think About

1. What is your view of defense mechanisms?

2. Do you understand a healthy defense mechanism?

3. When a couple is in a troubled relationship, why is it helpful to identify projection and projective identification?

4. Can you identify when you use denial as a defense?

5. How do you resolve the defense of resistance?

6. How is dissociation employed by sexual abuse survivors?

7. Have you identified triggers associated with trauma?

8. Are you working on resolving trauma responses?

9. Why is it important to accept lifestyle differences?

10. Do you keep up with the transgender advances in society?

What could love, the unsolved mystery, count for in the face of this possession of self-assertion which she suddenly recognized as the strongest impulse of her being?

—KATE CHOPIN, *The Story of an Hour*

CHAPTER III

What It Looks Like Now: The Challenge of Self-Care

PEOPLE SPEAK OF it being too late. Perhaps there are times when this is true, but too late for what? To change careers or to become something we've dreamt of? To become our internal dream means to stretch, to risk, to face the uncomfortable, to push through limits. Health concerns can confine us if we allow ourselves to become strangled by fear, yet many brave folks awaken us to what is possible by sharing their stories.

A woman with MS regulates chemotherapy to accommodate her working schedule. Another woman in recovery from breast cancer works one week on, one week off. A man post–prostate cancer decides not to take Viagra but rather to savor his time by furthering his passion for birding. A neighbor takes her mobile wheelchair two miles to the coffee shop. Unable to speak after a stroke, she orders her regular coffee and bagel.

Becoming what we never imagined may be possible. Life takes us to strongholds that make the unfathomed achievable, and courage can make the impossible happen. Disappointment can discourage the best of us, but our core harbors a spiritual floor, a respite from struggle, a pool of grace that is a springboard for transcending desperation. It resides internally and does not rely on false mythologies. The truest myths are our own deeply embedded personal territories. Ideas continue to flow like an endless river that empties into the ocean and back. Settling for just one life can feel limiting, but we can travel anywhere in our minds through the gift of imagination.

Inevitably, it takes us back to the present, reflecting on where we have been. Teasing out major and minor accomplishments thwarts the pull toward the negative, and gratitude erases resentments. Accessing the maven inside can lead us to our next adventure.

Myth

ALMOST IN A whisper, she recounts her conviction that a soul/spirit lives on forever in heaven. Her breathing changes from strained to relaxed as she tells herself a tale that calms her worries. Swollen with tumors, laden with an oxygen tank, her mate is carried by the will to survive another day. She sits by his side as he plays with their son. The boy speaks of life alone with mom; the three-year-old intuits this.

Her mythology of life and death does not work for me. I'll have to invent another story. The question is, What is your story? Do you need a hereafter? How do you self-calm when you worry or predict the future? Recently, I heard the word "oblivion." Do we stay oblivious to stay intact or in control. Is this okay? Maybe so—whatever works.

Nostalgia can be a powerful mechanism, but as I journey through my day, I try to *decide* just how much of the past I want to think about. Staying in the present helps me remain grounded. Dwelling on the "good old days" deflects me from what is right under my nose. Many of my clients want to anticipate the future; sometimes this invokes fears that may not play out. I ask them to be in their bodies for the day and manage their thoughts when they become too negative or begin predicting wretched results. A woman wants to know if her partner will ever change. She asks me, "Will he always be like this?" This question keeps her from staying present and actually observing/

experiencing how he is now, how he treats her. A circular argument is triggered in both of them, and she is blinded by her own mistakes, her responses to him. She blames herself for not being able to "win" an argument. The power trips between them keep her from taking responsibility for her participation in a never-ending battle. Each thinks the other should change. She doesn't want to give up on the relationship and thinks she wants to grow and change with this person, but she cannot stop worrying about whether he will change. Developmentally, people can and do change because life insists on adjustments. I try, however, to help her see what is in front of her and stay attuned to her instincts and ways of knowing.

Staying in the Day

I FEEL A prevailing sadness since the loss of my son. Each day, I awaken and make a list of what I want to accomplish. This gets me out of bed and on my way. The half-awake, half-asleep state brings confusion and a heaviness many elders speak of. What terrific role models they make as they practice listening to self-enhancement audiobooks on rising or writing their gratitude lists for the day. Controlling dark thoughts and worries about adult children and grandchildren is crucial. I don't use the term "shadow" thoughts; rather, I try to stay mindful of what I am thinking and practice ways to chase away unhelpful thoughts.

My mother was an elder most of my life until she died at eighty-six; I was forty-two. She would comment on what a miracle it was to have witnessed so many changes in her lifetime: the invention of the car, the telephone, freeways, air travel. Today, technology has taken us to new levels of communication, and these would fascinate her. I love to listen to elders and the way they use email,

Facebook, and cell phone cameras. Of course, there's the group that feels too befuddled to try these "gadgets," but for others, these lines of communication have radically changed people's ability to stay in social networks, helping to combat depression and isolation.

Sometimes the past is so looming it is difficult to stay in the present, to look around and feel grateful for one's life. Most people get a kick out of discovering an antique item or stumbling across an album with old photos. Many of these experiences will be lost to future generations with the advent of digital pictures and letters. Everything comes back around, and I suspect that will be true of this era. Someone will realize the past needs to be preserved. Elders like to tell their stories; there are websites where we can trace our lineage. It is powerful and empowering to discover those who came before us. What a privilege this is. Consider Serbia, North Africa, Bosnia, Cambodia, and the destruction of the villages and records of their personal and political histories. It is essential that we appreciate what we have and honor our ancestors. On the other hand, enough reflection is enough, I tell my aging clients.

Depression

THERE IS A push among the elderly to "get rid of things." Maybe their adult children express concern about their "stuff," or the elder may be concerned about leaving the clearing-out task to their children. So many speak of not wanting to be a "burden" to their kids. My nose wrinkles at this expression, and I reflect on my mother as she reached the end of her life. She had suffered a stroke and spent her last four years in a nursing facility. She acted as a model of acceptance with most of her children, but with me, she could reach some level of honesty. I am the youngest and probably one of the most challenging. During one of my visits with her, she looked around her room and said, "Your sister put me here, now she can take care of me." Ironically, the daughter she spoke of was most loving and willing to be there for her. I think of her words when I hear "burden" because it seemed she wasn't concerned when she made that crack to me. Before my father died four years prior, he was never concerned with being a burden—he expected to be taken care of. After all, this was exactly what my mother and his daughters had always done.

My mother was depressed when she made this remark to me. Perhaps that tad bit of anger helped ease the mood for a short time. Anger is a mobilizer and an important emotion, one we should not fear but rather view as helping us reach a deeper understanding of what needs to be addressed and changed. I like to help my clients make the distinction between anger and rage. People express that they don't like to be angry. At one point, a therapist told me my anger had saved me throughout my life. It was a defense that worked well for me. What a wise insight this was, and it has enabled me to help others feel the honesty of their anger.

A circle of elders gathered to talk about growing older. This helped with the loneliness and fear that goes with loss, illness, aching bones, and other challenges. The push toward isolation was temporarily lifted and new strengths discovered. The facilitator encouraged them to reflect on their early childhood. Some family systems themes surfaced: the eldest had felt responsibility for their parents and siblings. Many had served as the head of the family because of dysfunctional parents. They expressed being "fed up" with the role and wanted to be left alone. That attitude increased their isolation, and it became clear it was time to reach out and be helped instead of serving as the helper.

The middle children continually sought out support, often overburdening their families, yet they felt abandoned by their adult children. In the group, they learned about boundaries and alternative ways to seek support, often leaving their children out of the loop in their activities. The disabled sought out local services that enabled them to better function on their own. Several of these elders had left their biological families at an early age and entered relationships with the same attitude of being taken care of. Their tales of disappointment offered important lessons for the group as they developed patterns of support without encouraging dependency.

The youngest in the families often function like the oldest, depending on the age span between the siblings. They appeared to stay the most connected with their families of origin and often continue to be helpful to their adult children. They express fear of abandonment and find satisfaction in being needed.

As the youngest of eight with a twenty-four-year span between the oldest and me, I spent a lot of time alone. I filled the gap by organizing slumber parties and attaching myself to easygoing girlfriends whom I could coerce to stay with me. Later on, I became a leader of social activities in high school and in my early marriage. In my late twenties and later as a community organizer and social activist, I was continually busy with meetings, interventions, protests, and initiating programs for women and their children. Cushioned by my three children, I never really had to deal with loneliness. Now, as an elder, I am mindful of the feelings that surface when I am transitioning from one activity to another. It is a gut reaction that is old and hearkens back to when I was little and alone. I recall having only two books. Photos show me snuggling up to my sister, just under four years older than me. This age difference showed up early; she, too, received little attention from our parents and thus gravitated toward her friends.

Back to the Maven

THE MAVEN IS an expert, one who knows. Understanding that we cannot know everything can offer relief and help us acknowledge what we do know. Midlife ushers in the onset of many questions, including a search for change. This may involve a switch to another field of work; some begin talking about retirement, which is a signal that transition is about to happen. I then ask the questions, "How is burnout driving these feelings? Is there a mood shift that needs to be worked through?" Often at midlife, the person is a maven or expert who feels there's no more to learn. Embracing what we do know, however, leads us to serving others, who continue to learn from us.

Midlife introduces fears of mortality; it is a time when elder parents are dying or ill. Introspection about values, what we believe, is internal work, and changing the outside may not provide satisfaction. Marriages are under scrutiny at this time. Partners may have changed without the other's awareness, and resistance to that change is normal. Some stayed together as they raised their kids and now come face to face without those distractions. This can be a wonderful time for renewal but also frightening because old patterns don't work anymore. It may be time to face the stagnant nature of the relationship and start anew. People really do know when it is over, even though long-term relationships are generally revered. In turn, growing older together can be rewarding, even without the charge of the earlier relationship. It always makes me sad to see a young person stay in a relationship for financial purposes despite knowing they cannot be happy with or feel valued by their partner. Some elders, on the other hand, face critical financial stressors in leaving their relationships, and helping them stay and take care of themselves is the counselor's work.

Psychotherapy demands much personal growth, so the staying power of this profession is compelling. The learning curve never ends, and the feeling of truly being useful is fulfilling. In times of personal stress, witnessing the trials and successes of others helps the helper move out of personal pain. You know you have made a difference, and that is the mission of my life. Life with meaning sustains the wretchedness of loss, suffering, major changes, and challenges.

Years ago, I created a rubber stamp that reads, "Working for Change Is Greater Than Change Itself." I am talking about working for internal as well as external change. I ask, What are the material conditions of your life, and what has to change there? What are the internal conditions that need to change? Is moving out of a relationship going to change the results of your internal condition? Is staying in the relationship going to change the results of the internal condition? Does moving into a new career mean there will be change in the internal life? Or does staying in your work mean challenging and changing your inner life?

Self-Care

PEOPLE MAKE EXCUSES for not taking care of themselves. Sometimes this makes me laugh, which isn't the best reaction when I am observing defenses against self-care. I guess it is easy for me to make suggestions given that I have built in time for daily walks, playing my guitar, and writing songs and poems. When bosses don't value their employees enough to make sure they are taking breaks or lunch hours, people must advocate for themselves. Given the landmark work unions have accomplished in this country, the right to balance in the workplace is elementary. The physical cost of not taking care is too high.

A client who recovered from cancer a year ago now continues the same patterns back on the job. My responsibility is to help her make the connections between her illness and habits of self-neglect. It can be difficult to take that walk at lunchtime and eat at her desk because her supervisor subtly frowns on this practice. Her resolve must be to put herself first, to stay within the confines of the work and figure out a way to take better care, whether that means taking a walk with the dog, working out at the gym, eating more vegetables and fruit, or practicing yoga. There are so many options for self-care. True, this can be challenging if you are struggling with depression or anxiety. Medications may be helpful, but releasing endorphins through exercise can also treat symptoms. I stress breathing from the intestines, where dopamine and serotonin are housed. These can help regulate brain activity and fend off depression.

Since 9/11 and the constant news of terrorism, the rise in anxiety has become obvious. PTSD in veterans has surfaced as a crisis. Pharmacological companies have flourished as a primary treatment, and counseling has reached a new level of respect. We recognize that drug therapy without psychotherapy, dialectical behavioral programs, and support groups is a limited approach. Experiencing consistent advocacy and having backups work. Veterans are speaking out about poor services, and family support is necessary to help members adjust to times of great stress and fear.

This is not to say psychotropic medications are unnecessary interventions. Antidepressants and anti-anxiety prescriptions can help keep clients functional. We all hear horror stories about prescription drug addiction, but when they are used properly with good medical guidance, people can benefit.

One Day at a Time

MY MOTHER USED to say, "Don't wish your life away." I guess this was her answer to my grumbling, wanting something to be different. She used to tell me she was old enough to be my grandmother when I became too much for her to handle. I knew then it was an excuse to distance herself from me. Indeed, it must have been challenging to give birth to another child at the age of forty-five, but I can still get in touch with the anger I felt when she checked out on me. For all my awareness of her fatigue and my feeling like I was a drag on her, I did pay attention to her pearls of wisdom. Now, I find myself murmuring those tips myself. Today, I don't wish my life away, and I help clients take life a one day at a time.

An alcoholic woman in early recovery is having a tough time staying sober. I can tell she is often suicidal, but she doesn't express that. She is restless and cannot think of ways to fill her day since leaving her job. I stress that her job now is self-care, attending AA meetings, and being there for another alcoholic. She has spent the last twenty years in a highly intense administrative position and cannot imagine what a person does all day without work. Angry and resistant, she says she does not like AA meetings. I suggest that is her way back to a drink. She doesn't like this confrontation but agrees to try to go to more meetings. How far gone is our culture that we cannot understand self-care is our real job? Granted, it took me a long time to realize this myself, and I forget on occasion when I binge on a dessert. Oh well, nobody's perfect, I tell myself. What a good thing that is: I don't have to be perfect.

My partner works with drug addicts. Some are women who have lost their children, gotten sober, had another child, and then lost that one to child welfare. Ominous is the challenge of sobriety when we have lost an entire network of support. Even in the depths of their substance use, these women still had a way to belong, to be a part of something bigger. I am in awe of workers like my partner, Marie, who hang in there no matter what. Taking care of herself under this kind of stress is challenging. Regression is often a feature in getting clean and sober, but the strength of the counselors and case managers who continually restore hope is remarkable. When we see the homeless who are addicted panhandling for money, we either feel judgment or compassion or both. The vacillation between those feelings can be exhausting for the workers.

In the past, I was hesitant to work with people who were still using substances. After one session, it became obvious the price for giving up the "best friend" of alcohol or drugs was high. Sober folks will say some people just don't "get it." But intuitively, they do get it. They know they will have to change their thinking, their habits, their support base. The transformational work required to move beyond the impulse-driving nature of addiction means facing an unknown, and that is frightening. Even though the brain chemistry says we cannot live without satisfying the compulsion, it comes down to choice and discipline, plus a good support system.

The addiction field is changing. Hardliners who took the position of no drinking no matter what understand that can only work to a point. Most counselors set small, realizable goals with their clients and believe sobriety can happen over time. This ideology has impacted my work in that I can literally sit back and wait for clients to make the connection between their drinking and the fact that their lives are moving backward. Reminding them of this plus telling them I am there waiting is helpful to an extent. In reality, many will leave therapy until they face these realizations on their own.

Stumbling into other addictions is also part of the process. One man speaks of his inability to leave the computer during most of his free time. Facebook and Twitter hold him spellbound. He feels connected there while slowly beginning to experience the ill health that comes from no exercise and bad eating habits. Add smoking to the straps of the computer chair, and this is a heart attack in the works. Clearly, significant change must occur for this man to save himself.

Paradoxically, some therapists ask others to do what they cannot do for themselves. That was me for a long time. I legitimized my drinking by only drinking in the evenings. I helped others get sober while denying I needed to confront my own lifestyle. At the time, I was involved in a relationship with someone I regarded as a passing connection. This lasted four-and-a-half years with many breakups. Alcohol kept me in the relationship as I stayed for the companionship of drinks and dinner at a favorite restaurant. My biggest clue that I needed to stop drinking was when I realized how much I was looking forward to a martini after work.

Many physicians suffer a similar dilemma in that they have automatic access to prescription drugs. Because they have seen drugs ease pain for others, it may seem logical to treat themselves with drug therapy as they face stresses in their own lives. Doctors everywhere are speaking more freely about their addictions and welcome monitoring to help them get to the other side of their afflictions. One physician friend speaks of his treatment, which lasted six months at a clinic designed to treat doctors. He expresses anguish as he recalls the number of fellow patients there who committed suicide. So much was at stake for my friend—he gave up his practice, borrowed money, and broke up his family system. In looking back, he has no doubt the pharmacist who turned him in saved his life.

Occasionally, I meet with a woman concerned about her partner's use of pornography. Male friends have told me it's normal for men to look at women's bodies and masturbate or maybe to just enjoy the view. This has been a helpful tip for me, and, over the years, I have softened my position. Of course, I don't want women to be exploited or be paid low wages for the use of their bodies for the pleasure of others. I listen to women's voices to guide me. If prostitution is involved, women need to be in control of managing their affairs as they are so vulnerable to the legal system. Pornography and prostitution may be a continuum, which is often why women react so strongly to the use of porn in their homes. One woman ultimately severed her relationship because she realized her husband was spending more time away from her and glued to the computer. When confronted, he chose his lifestyle over her.

Taking care of ourselves looks different for everyone. Living in a wheelchair entails creatively working with the upper body and keeping the circulation moving in the lower body. One friend cannot walk without extreme back pain, so he regularly works out at the gym; another woman goes to the gym every night after work to stay muscular. She likes that kind of body, even at the age of seventy. This same woman has toned down her love of the fast life to continue in her job, where she feels fulfilled. My daughter, Molly, cannot walk long distances, so she has agreed to use a wheelchair when she is on an outing. My generation was not taught to take care of ourselves, but today, staying fit is encouraged.

Questions to Think About

1. What are your views on coping with depression, including medications?

2. How do you describe the "maven" in you?

3. In what ways do you practice self-care?

4. How do you regulate nostalgia and reflection on the past?

5. Do you believe it is important to stay in the day in your actions and thoughts?

6. How do addictions affect people's lives, and what treatment is available?

7. Do you believe people can change? Do you believe you can change?

8. What changes are occurring in the addiction recovery field?

9. How would you assess your use of substances?

10. Would you reach out for help if you thought you had a problem?

Fate was both what we were given and what we made for ourselves.

—ALICE HOFFMAN, *The Museum of Extraordinary Things*

CHAPTER IV

Staying Positive in the Storm

THE SEARCH FOR "normal" seems universal. The question invariably surfaces: "Is that normal?" Normalizing symptoms is the most relieving response. While strolling down the street or enjoying a meal in a restaurant, we get the impression that the folks we see are the norm—and often unlike us. So much of life is an illusion, and we project onto others what we need to stay emotionally intact. The hidden reality, however, is people are tremendously stressed. How do we keep going under duress? The tools for taking life as it comes are not necessarily handed down from the original family. One teacher told me she begins each day with an exercise. She has first-graders put their heads on their desks and close their eyes. Then she takes them on a spiritual quest in their imaginations. She started this practice many years ago when she noticed how her students reflected the tension in their families. As a result, she was able to help students start the day grounded in their own reality, pushing away pressures from outside themselves. Strength lies within: this was the message.

In that vein, when I was first adjusting to the trauma of my son's death, I continually watched movies as an escape from unbearable pain. I searched these films for helpful messages. This was my way of finding teachers, people, and animals who inspired me. I heard a powerful message from a Native American character helping a coworker stay calm. "Clear your thoughts," he said. To clients who cannot settle their minds or stay in the present, I say, "Clear your thoughts." It is a powerful thought-stopping practice. I still use this when my mind is racing and I am trying to go to sleep.

Joseph Campbell's writings on myth and discovery of the hero inside have also impacted my writing. I remember when I first got sober, a therapist told me the higher power was in me—not coming from outside. I think she may have been employing some of Campbell's work. It helped me to awaken a goddess inside myself, one with higher power, allowing me to reach a state of grace. Campbell's teachings were based on our being one with the world as the source of all strength and awareness, providing healing. We can think of our traumas and sorrows as being wounds of the body and self. This enables us to heal ourselves with the help of others.

These are easy words to hear but difficult to believe when we are in the middle of the storm. For a year after Tom's departure from this world, I sought signs that he was still hovering. One day as I walked through a parking lot, I looked up at a birdie sitting in the single tree in the lot, and I said, "It's okay, you can come with me." Unbelievably, this starling landed on my shoulder for just a second, then flew off. Okay, I became a believer. Tom and I went birding, and whenever we were together, we paid attention to what the birds were doing. We discovered some remarkable achievements. One time, by one of our Rogue River spots, we encountered a giant pileated woodpecker pecking at an aging log. We were elated because of the rarity of this bird in our area. This is the spot where we later chose to spread Tom's ashes.

When someone dies, people try to be helpful by putting themselves in the other's shoes. Inevitably, this leads to advice like, "Go with the sadness. Walk through the pain. Talk about it. Join a group. Look at the photos. Cry if you need to." Every now and then, one of these lines is helpful. Another piece of advice is, "Everyone is different, and they grieve in their own way." That hits the nail on the head. Being in that state of traumatic shock with a loss so close to home means experiencing completely foreign emotions. Actually, nothing works. Another rap, "Time takes care of everything." This is true; we must continue on. But the will to go forward must be there. Despite the guilt of leaving the lost loved one behind, we must stay in our own life.

A client lost her mother and father within a single year. For a long time, all she could see around her was death. She became obsessed with aging, fearing change. Reading the obituaries was a way of passing time. She openly wept and roamed the streets, observing the wonder of nature. She was in constant conflict with her partner, who wanted her to make better progress in her bereavement. She instinctively knew she could not rush her process. This was her way of staying positive while feeling so wretched. She wanted to change everything in her life, maybe even her partner. Death was forcing her to push away all that reminded her of loss. I encouraged her to wait a year before making these decisions as she could not tease out whether these would be changes she would choose if not in her present state of mind. One realization that lingered after a year's time: she needed to quit her high-stress job and live her days differently. This is the lesson of mortality—we only have this life to live the way we know is best for our mental and physical health. Even if she chose to stay in her job, she would have to integrate ways to visit nature as she had during the early days of grieving.

Trauma impacts us in complex ways. Reading a Facebook entry that describes a sexual attack or a nonconsensual YouTube video of a sexual encounter changes a person's life. This needs to be followed up with a police report with the hope that the perpetrator will be held accountable.

Teen suicide is epidemic and often results from this kind of assault and humiliation. Suicide cannot become an option to stop the pain, but it is not always easy to detect when a victim is planning this way out. Monica Lewinsky, caught up in the Clinton scandal of the 1990s, has finally been able to surface, writing a book and reclaiming her life. Her mother encouraged her to write her story when she learned a young gay man had committed suicide after a video of him having sex was circulated around campus. Ms. Lewinsky's mother had sat next to her suicidal daughter for months after the tragic chain of events. This is now a healing for both mother and daughter.

Ideally, we can frame our experiences in a way that teaches us something meaningful or gives us hope so we can carry on. This innate instinct to survive may seem temporarily dormant, but then, like spring, an internal blooming of renewal and strength begins to surface. We realize we can create a revival or a new life that will take us forward. People talk about God as their source, and this has inspired me to search for some representation of this to surrender and relinquish my will to. I chose to internalize the Greek goddess Artemis. I identify with her as a strong-willed, independent goddess, a lover of wildlife who is a nurturer yet can also be vindictive. She goes to great lengths to protect nature and those she loves. She dances through the forests and mountains.

When I heard of Mrs. Lewinsky's vigilant protection of her daughter, the Greek goddess Demeter came to mind. In my Mothers and Daughters classes, I often talk about Demeter's eternal pursuit of her daughter, Persephone, whom Zeus had granted to evil Hades without Demeter's knowledge. While Hades held Persephone captive, Demeter's desperate grief created winter. For six months of the year, however, Demeter got Persephone back, and her joy blossomed into spring. The pain Demeter faced in this trade was tremendous, and it speaks to the pain we feel when our daughters go astray. Like Demeter, we must wait until they return from hell and rejoin us. Demeter is also known for her love of the earth's gifts of nature. She is complex in her own right and more than a mother.

My daughter, Brigid, has assumed a protective role as caretaker and companion to her sister, Molly. She often plays the role of Demeter, providing safety for her sister. When Brigid lost her own way, I had to wait for her return without hovering, keeping my boundaries intact. This did not always go well and was the most painful for us when we were not as close. Daughters, in their internalization of their mothers, tend to keep the mother within an emotionally short distance. I love the image of the daughter looking over her shoulder to ensure her mother, like Demeter, is present, symbolically within reach. This is how mothers, in turn, stay strong, knowing our daughters will always return.

Anger

IN MY OFFICE, I keep two photos of me as a child. In one, I am about three years old, happily playing with my truck on the driveway. The second was taken when I was six or seven, and my face shows how upset I was. I was angry with my mother by that time, mostly because I knew she didn't make time to be with me. She was not a mother who played with her children. Perhaps mothers at that time were not encouraged to do so. She liked to swim, so we swam together; she liked to ice-skate, so we skated together. She liked to dance, and I often was on the dance floor with her later in our lives. I keep the pictures in my office to remind me of the transitions in early childhood and how painful they can be. As mentioned earlier, a therapist once told me my anger had saved me and this defense had pulled me through hard times. It was then I learned to respect anger as part of the range of human emotions.

Mary has healthy access to her anger and at times cannot let go of her perspective when processing with her partner; he is continually critical of her. Our work has been to help her regulate her emotions to match the situation. Mary came to do some individual work with the hope that she could change. Admittedly, she is the kind of person I tend to like, understand, and identify with. It all goes back to the photo of me as a seven-year-old. My anger is that old, even with all the work I have done to alleviate that painful emotion, and I understand where my client is coming from. I respect her anger and her perspective. Change does not mean giving up her anger but rather respecting her inner messages, figuring out the best way to honor her instincts and self-regulate.

Combating the Dread

On awakening, the "dread" often sets in. Perhaps anxiety prevents us from sleeping. Racing thoughts manifest as worrying late at night when we're weary or when we first wake up. The treatment is to practice relaxation and change our thoughts, setting up a list of activities for the day ahead. When fear takes over, we must remember we are more than our thoughts and we are not defined by our work, children, or partners. We are independent beings who seek connection; we are capable of taking control of our lives while at the same time are seeking ways to give up control.

I used to characterize myself as fearless, and this was true when I faced a car accident that marred my face and took my front teeth. This was true when I designed an elaborate program for rehabilitation of my daughter, Molly; when I faced divorce, deciding to raise my children as a single mother; when I returned to school at thirty-one; and when I moved to Boston and set up a private practice. It was only when I stopped drinking that I faced fear, perhaps for the first time. Post-menopausal symptoms collided with becoming sober. I became fearful and had to figure out what to do about it. Now, as an elder, the fear can become profound at times, and I am working through this sometimes on an hourly basis. I have learned not to be concerned about my fear but to view it as a part of this life stage. The greatest gift I can give my elderly clients is to identify with them and help them normalize the emotions connected with age and mortality.

My community consists of many communities, including a food co-op that offers organic foods but also elevated prices. People of privilege abide, and the homeless circulate freely, often on the steps of the co-op. Their presence makes my heart heavy, and apparently it pays for them to hang out at the store because the tidings are plenty. My friend at the hardware store is upset by the dominant presence of the homeless and suggests people hand out money because they feel guilty. Contradictions exist everywhere in a class-bound society rooted in capitalist ideology. I am embarrassed by and become agitated at some of the local bumper stickers like "The best things in life aren't things." What nerve to say this when material belongings can mean the difference between life and death for those who have no access to resources. What is the implication here? Does this mean that if we have met all the stages of Maslow's hierarchy of needs, then we can contemplate the meaning of life? At the bottom of Maslow's hierarchy is food, clothing, and housing. These are essential needs. At the top of the hierarchy, "meaning" was added in the 1940s by Psychologist Viktor E. Frankl. This is an ambitious goal in a culture that rewards wealth and punishes poverty.

You don't have to be poor to be attached to things. When I look at my windowsill and observe birdies at the feeder, I feel grateful that I have the feeder! I treasure the figurine my mother passed down to me. True, most things are replaceable, but I sure like hanging on to some favorites, like the car we drive, the television we use to view our favorite DVDs, and the computer I am writing this book on. Gratitude for the things in my life supplants longing, the desire to fill an internal hole that cannot be satisfied by goods. When we watch the writhing pain of families who have lost their homes to floods, raging fires, tornados, or hurricanes, we witness their gratitude for being alive while at the same time they are grieving the loss of their earthly goods.

The issue of homelessness seems unsolvable as society attempts to find a way to handle the visible manifestation of something very wrong. Programs galore exist but cannot touch the reality that our political and social systems depend on inequity. All of my adult life, I have worked to end this wretched reality, and only slight changes have been made within the larger picture. It is hard not to become discouraged. My activist life, however, led me to where I am today as a social worker with the degrees to enable me to feel elements of success.

Intuition has always been my guide. If we pay attention, we realize we already know the answers to our own questions. This does not mean we can solve every riddle or always notice how we effect change. When working in an individual or group counseling setting, we often witness personal transformation. These are thrilling moments, satisfying and significant when assessing whether we can make a difference. It may mean no longer demonstrating in the streets but instead valuing another's personal path to change and keeping up with the online chatter everyone depends on now for feedback. Sometimes this means helping others define themselves not by their work or relationships or status in life. For me, defining myself by my work is compelling. Sometimes after a long weekend or vacation, I welcome being back in the "little room." Returning to my work reminds me of what I do best and what I am like when I am at my best. Much personal change happens there in the circle between us. We are both changed as a result of our sitting together. I get it when people really love their work and feel loss when they are not embroiled in it. We say work is not our life, but it is so much a part of our life that minimizing its impact does not help us address the balance we need to achieve.

More Self-Care

SLOWING DOWN AND taking it easy seems like an oxymoron when we experience a speedy feeling as we move through tasks and our day. We watch women and men multitask as they try to keep ahead of the demands of their day. Get the child to daycare on time, drop the kids at school, stop at the grocery store, think through the evening meal, get to the soccer game on time. Yikes! How does all this get done, with the last stop being yoga after work? Slow down. I guess that's where it happens— at a yoga session or a gym workout. This is an ideal way to tend to the body and mind. Yet many cannot afford the cost of a gym membership or a daily yoga session, or their schedules make it impossible. The cost of extended daycare often makes this out of the question. It gets down to finding simple ways to exercise or practice calming.

Walking a dog with the kids is a common practice, and preparing meals in advance or ordering food helps. Over time, each family must address the dilemma of hustle and bustle in their daily lives.

I listen to the hype about eating the right foods and avoiding the wrong foods and remember how difficult it was to not give in to my children at the grocery checkout line as they beg for a candy bar or whatever temptation was staring them in the face. Co-op shopping makes it easier to manage this, but many cannot afford the luxury of buying healthy food. The emphasis on family farms and sustainable living is easing our food worries but has a long way to go before it trickles down to families with low incomes. Again, how can we help those who are without incomes, homeless, or have no access to human services practice self-care?

There is much we can do nothing about, so where do we begin to make a difference in our lives and the lives of others? We can begin right where we are, staying in the day and focusing on what is in front of us. Mindfulness is a helpful practice in that it starts with concentration on what is going on in our bodies. The message of the moment lies there. Practicing ways to stay aware helps: tapping our clavicle area or ribs, rubbing our shoulders, putting our feet up for a spell, and checking our thoughts to make sure they match the situation. We can pay attention to our walking, always conscious when we are carrying things. Mostly, we need to stop the intrusive worrying about the future or obsessing over resentments. It can be fun and helpful to brainstorm with ourselves, but we must make a conscious decision to do so without distractions that could lead us to accidents.

Journaling or writing notes to ourselves helps us channel feelings and ideas in an organized way. Julia Cameron's book *The Artist's Way* walks readers through the "morning papers" as a powerful way to become more aware of our personal process. This text is a terrific tool for facilitating a path to the creative person within.

Remaining mindful of our moods, we must make sure we are not projecting our irritability onto others. Swearing at another driver in the privacy of our car is a good way to let off steam and is seemingly harmless. As the day wears on, weariness sets in. Note the lessons of babies: naps save the day. Whether we take the time to rest, paying attention to what is going on inside when edginess is present will prevent us from becoming upset with our partners. Counseling provides a space to learn about mindfulness, but we don't always remember to practice this in our relationships.

Jennifer, a client her partner termed "high-maintenance," began taking responsibility for her irritability over time. Her intensity, however, was what had drawn her partner to her in the first place. He was invested in the dynamic between them and had to accept his part in the emotions of the relationship, and he actually did not want her to change. Eventually, they reached a compromise. Jennifer toned down her delivery but stayed confident in herself. Her depth of insight enabled her to analyze what was going on, and Jennifer needed to stop expecting these same strengths from her partner. He was loving and supportive but often did not understand the ramifications of his comments and behaviors. For me, this became a simple case in that Jennifer needed to accept him and appreciate what he was able to contribute. In time, he learned to ask for her guidance when he needed to learn something about the complex nature of Jennifer.

Beloved Buddhist teacher Thích Nhất Hạnh shares this advice: "The most precious gift we can offer anyone is attention. When mindfulness embraces those we love, they will bloom like flowers."

Destiny

THE HOLIDAYS BRING mixed feelings: families gathering together, glad to arrive and anxious to leave. Christmas cards display photos of multiple children and grandchildren. People send these as a source of pride, proud they have produced new generations, but sometimes these presentations bring regret and sadness for me. I have no grandchildren, but I do get to spend time with my two special daughters and wonderful partner. Being content with what is can be challenging.

I recently talked about my destiny with my daughter, Molly, who suffered brain injury at birth and is multiply-handicapped. I joked that I was picked by the heavens to be her mother, her guardian, the person who knows her. Her sister, Brigid, knows her. I do not have grandchildren; I have Molly. She is my destiny. This is what I was meant to do. I have always known this, even when I felt sorry for myself.

This leads me to ask, What is your destiny? There is much talk about determining your own destiny and, indeed, this has merit. But I am asking what is the destiny determined not by you but by a force of life outside yourself? Sometimes we don't have a choice. How does this apply to you?

Staying positive in the storm can work by allowing us to focus on the smallest aspect of ourselves, our culture, the earth, and the amazing resiliency of human nature.

As I planted my garden this past year, I turned over the soil and added soil enhancements and a fragrant cocoa combination. It's a small plot with a poor track record, but I persevere. I planted tomatoes, cucumbers, peppers, strawberries, lettuce, basil, and pumpkins. What I didn't add was sunflowers. Soon after planting and before any other growth, up came little green sprouts. Lots of them. I started plucking them from the dirt, but then decided to wait and see what would happen to the remaining ones. *Voilà*—sunflowers! The seeds had lain dormant for over a year. After I moved the soil around, they found a safe, comfortable place to show their faces. One is the largest plant in the garden, as if standing guard to ward off critters strolling through the property. What I thought I had control over was not entirely true, and life always brings me a surprise. This is a sweet realization that holds me through the day as I listen to the pain and suffering as well as the joys of peoples' lives.

Questions to Think About

1. Can you identify the personal strengths you draw on when stressed?

2. How would you define a state of grace?

3. Do you observe the forces of nature around you?

4. What changes do you need to make?

5. How would you describe a mother/daughter bond?

6. Do you believe anger is a valid emotion?

7. How would you describe your daily rituals?

8. What material goods do you treasure?

9. In what ways do you practice self-care?

10. Do you practice mindfulness?

Made direct amends to such people whenever possible, except when to do so would injure them or others.

—STEP IX, 12 STEPS OF ALCOHOLICS ANONYMOUS

CHAPTER V

Clearing Mistakes, Making Amends

WHEN SAYING WE'RE sorry the question surfaces, Who is this helping? The amender or the amendee? It feels good when people apologize to those they've offended. I recall when my sister apologized for axing me out of her life for two years. I immediately said "Okay," and we moved into our next activity. We liked to do a lot of the same things then: demonstrations, political meetings, shopping, viewing historical sites. Now I ask why was I so eager to accept her apology? Why did I need so badly to be back in her good graces? Perhaps it was because she was in the wrong, and it was my role to stand aside and wait for her return. It was remarkable that she was able to admit her bad judgment, but she knew I would always come back to her. Today, this rings true, even though much has separated us since that time.

Many of us have had to sever relationships yet struggle with how to resume contact. This poses a dilemma because in reality it may be unwise to do this. It means understanding what would be the benefit of reconnection, figuring out what they would want, gauging the wear and tear of relating to them, and judging whether it would be healthy to resume. It may be hard to admit that it may not work out if you have been a fixer all your life, often putting yourself aside for others, still retaining a certain amount of integrity and honesty. Perhaps you must reconcile yourself to believing that in time things will all get worked out, without taking control and trying to do what your body is indicating you cannot handle.

As a starting point, we can make amends with ourselves. It is not easy to recall the ways in which we hurt others if we defended against accepting responsibility during those times. For those of us raised in a religious environment, guilt and shame were part of the program. I picture twenty little third-graders bowing their heads while listening to stories of sinful ways and feeling badly about themselves, fearful they are headed down the path of evil. Undoing these guilt trips as adults can take years. Guilt is a worthless emotion unless it drives us to do something to resolve the issue. For me, guilt works with teens and can be a helpful factor in combating temptations to do what they know is unwise or self-destructive. Most of all, kids need to understand people suffer when they act out and get into trouble with parents, teachers, and others who care about them. This is a tall order for adolescents, who do not feel loved or particularly cared for. Vulnerable kids are naturally gullible and can easily become involved with a bad crowd. If awareness of their loved ones is there, however, they often can resist pressure to engage in risky or criminal behavior. What to do about those who are lost remains society's dilemma. Every family has a built-in value system, and overtly imparting those standards influences children, even if it means repeating the important messages over and over. This recording plays out when kids are tempted to cross into dangerous territory. If they stray, saying they are sorry and making amends makes a difference. This act can erase residual feelings.

It is never too late. A young mother has lost three children to the child welfare system. Many attempts at sobriety have ended in heartbreaking loss. With the last baby, it seemed as though she would be able to keep the child, but unsettled breaches with her parole officer enabled the state to take her child. The despair this young mother feels triggers another round of drug and alcohol abuse, and the cycle completes itself by the loss of another baby. Focusing on the strengths she used during her sober times is a clue that eventually she may be able to recapture a life in which she can accept her trials and thrive. All of her older children long for her return as each have been challenged by the child welfare system. While the details of this case history are overwhelming to contemplate, life continues, and we have to believe one day things will change for this family. Some of the results feel predictable as the children navigate the foster care system and end up like their parents. Once we fall into predictive thinking, however, despair becomes contagious and must be fought against.

Deepak Chopra teaches "peace is the way." His writings are lessons in meditation, reaching for a calm and meaningful life. His practices have been helpful for many. When we listen to the news, we wonder why these principles have fallen on deaf ears. It is commonplace for us to respond to an inner violent, defensive nature when we listen daily to episodes of violence everywhere in the world. When we learn of Al Qaeda attacks, Taliban activities, and the destructive actions of certain leaders, many of us cry out, "Just take them out!" Our anger and sense of powerlessness over politics drive this response, but when we realize this means taking a life, we are surprised at our gut reaction. People of my generation do not remember so much violence surrounding our everyday lives. Yet our parents lived through the Depression, two world wars, and several more wars after that. There was violence everywhere, but it wasn't under everyone's noses, and we were spared the daily media onslaught. Even during the Civil Rights protests and killings, the media coverage was limited. Life is more complicated now, and it is certainly an uphill battle. I laugh, thinking, no wonder people watch *Dancing with the Stars*, *The Bachelor*, and other get-away-from-it-all programs. We sometimes need to duck our heads into the sand and become ostriches to cope with the frustration and anger at the stupidity of leadership.

The question becomes, What is the role of forgiveness in all of this? As Americans, we cannot easily understand tribal ritual and ideology, even though each of us is a part of our own tribe. We speak of laying down our lives to save a child in danger or rescue someone in an emergency. Our first responders and military personnel certainly manifest this practice. If we think of this more on a global scale, maybe then we can better understand Arab and Middle Eastern cultural values. When we see the Egyptian or Syrian protesters gathered by the thousands, risking their lives in search of a better world, we get a glimpse of tribal culture. Suicide bombings in markets, hotels, and village squares feel harsh and are not easily grasped by our American minds. These actions, however, are perceived as an ultimate sacrifice or retaliation for injustices. Here, we revere individual freedoms, but often also work collectively for change—just not in this suicidal fashion. Protest has always been part of the American way.

What is the point here? Can we understand and forgive those we do not relate to or understand? Can we forgive ourselves when our country wipes out whole villages in the name of defending other countries? Is this a form of protection for our own freedom? It is billed that way, and many of us really do not understand the ideology of war and killing, which puts us in a bind. We judge Muslim and Arab practices such as killing for a larger cause. Our country has eliminated villains like Osama bin Laden;

we have executed terrorists. As we negotiate tradeoffs of prisoners from Iran, Iraq, and Russia, how do we justify supporting decisions that may ultimately be dangerous for our country?

If we watch the national news, we see more multi-cultural narrators and reporters on hostile assignments. Sometimes people ask where the white people are. Certainly, we hear this question freely asked on more conservative stations. What an illuminating experience to listen to broadcasters whose names we cannot easily pronounce. In addition, multiracial has replaced biracial as a common descriptor. These historical breakthroughs are powerful, and we do not know where this will take us as a country with our own tribal issues.

In his film, *Thrive: What on Earth Will It Take*, Foster Gamble defines "thrive" as the natural flow of life. Nature is a "self-organizing system" that will continue to heal injuries to our planet. This process, he warns, is thwarted by eugenics through the use of toxins that render men infertile and destroy towns and countries.

The conservationists are a wonderful source of hope and an example of how the earth continues to forgive the abuses of human folly. Working in communities on waterways, wetlands, pastures, and forest, The Nature Conservancy has purchased six million acres to protect ecological communities. This fast-growing movement, acutely aware of the impact of climate change and its ram-ifications, has identified probabilities of species responses to loss of habitant through floods, scorched crops, and dried-up water sources. They are observing adaptability of insects, birds, and other life forms as they find sustain-able life in new structures such as higher rock formations like serpentine, rich with the mineral life needed to sur-vive. Humans are discovering more species are managing to forgive the mistakes of human beings and their inability to care for Mother Earth.

Native American communities have been reaching out to the president with hopes that he will act on their concerns about the impact of oil line tunnels, which require digging up their lands and using up their water. Such practices are leading to the extinction of fish and wildlife, with little knowledge of how this will ultimately play out.

Our ability to forgive depends on what it is we are up against and how we are reminded of the hurt we have experienced.

A friend is on her third marriage. She says she likes to get married. It's not the first time I've heard this. Many of us take marriage seriously, while others keep moving on to the next partner. This is common among the unmarried, and we often expect that. The more partners we end up with, however, the more people they bring with them. Just when someone thinks they have found the right person, they inherit a whole tribe. This works well if one likes large families, but it can be an issue if the partner's children are part of the package.

It wasn't until after the third marriage that my friend found out her beloved had two children with whom he'd had no previous contact. Both a son and daughter ended up living close by, sometimes bunking with my friend and her twins by her new partner. First, she resented her partner not clueing her in on his long-lost children's existence; second, she became angry every time they appeared in her living room. In anger, she gave her partner an ultimatum—either her or them. He held his ground and said he would not give up his children, now that he had just reconnected with them. This was important to him. When my friend's blackmail didn't work, she began to distance from her partner, often sobbing late into the night. Even then he didn't budge. Nothing seemed to work in their relationship anymore, even if she left the house when the children were there.

My friend had to confront her pattern of moving in and out of marriages to avoid going through hard times. She is now developing ways to stay close to her husband, respect his choices, and understand this challenge as an opportunity to change.

International Forgiveness

IN EUROPE, THE conservation movement is developing rapidly, with farmers setting up reserves for endangered birds and animal life, figuring out the impact of re-wilding herbivores, reintroducing species like wild horses and red deer, and letting predators thrive to balance ecosystems of the past. The organizations that create programs to fund ambitious enterprises like wilderness rebirths barely leak into American media. Letting nature take its own course is not a viable ideology, given that nature has been so radically altered by human activity as well as animal life in pursuit of sustenance. Anytime there is a dialectical process, there will be resistance. Much is driven by profit-seekers, but small populations of farmers and people trying to feed their families fear the changes and sacrifices involved. Supporting them is a big part of the work. Conservationists need to be aware of the impact of their actions. Forgiveness involves reaching out and listening to the real concerns of the populace.

Forgiving ourselves is a direct line to acceptance of our history. As we ponder the things we would change if we had the opportunity, sadness and self-criticism surface. Simply saying you cannot change the past doesn't always take away the regret. We want a do-over. A woman is concerned about a sexually transmitted disease she contracted from a few nights of passion with a man she barely knew. They got drunk together, and things progressed from there. They had fun, but it didn't last, and she is filled with rage at him for not protecting her from this venereal disease. Moreover, she blames herself and wants a do-over. In working through her despair, she was able to confront the man, who denied being infected. She asks, "So, where did that get me?" She did what she had to do but is still stuck with the lingering feelings of self-judgment. Somehow she needed to grasp that as a young person, she will have sexual encounters as part of her exploration of sexuality. This is not an unusual lifestyle. "Hookups" are common practice and facilitated by social networks. Deciding whether to drop out of that scene is inevitable now for this woman. She wants to address her drinking patterns, take relationships more seriously, and not infect another person. Treating and managing her condition and forgiving herself are her priorities.

AIDS

IN VIEWING LARRY Kramer's play *The Normal Heart*, many emotions surfaced as I was taken back to my time in Boston. Out as a lesbian just two years, I was swept into Boston lesbian and gay politics and elected chair of the Lesbian, Gay, Bisexual Political Alliance (Transgender was added later) as the community was going through the devastation of AIDS. In my twelve years there, I lost my best political allies, personal friends, and professional colleagues. As the play so aptly portrays, we lived in a continually dazed state, not understanding what was happening and with no hope of a cure in sight. Miraculously, the community fought against its demise, confronting political figures from the president to state officials. With the background of hate and discrimination against gays and lesbians, most of the time we were like mice caught in a cage, going round and round, with no perceivable end. Dead figures lying all around us. We would attend a meeting with activists one day, only to find them missing and dead the next.

In the meantime, I was caught up in the adversity experienced by those facing death in the wake of an HIV diagnosis and others tending to dying partners. Many of these individuals were engaged in power trips over control of leadership. I only came to understand much of the tension later as I stepped out of the limelight. Lesbians had taken over many roles originally held by men, confronting sexism in the political ranks of the community. Men had to concede and work with women, who had also started a movement to create families by way of insemination. Support groups swelled as hundreds of lesbians joined, and their voices grew stronger when they began having children.

A health center was established to serve a population of men living with HIV/AIDS and pregnant women. The AIDS Action Committee took in numerous activists who under normal circumstances would have been picketing and working for a gay and lesbian rights bill. Yet, even with all this, the Lesbian, Gay, Bisexual, Rights Bill was passed. We celebrated and grieved simultaneously.

Much of the political work meant exposing politicians who were not paying attention to the onslaught of dying gay men, including President Reagan and Congress members who refused to institute policies and resources to help the gay community contend with the fast-moving disease. Larry Kramer led the way in naming those in office who would not listen. As a society, we really have no way to make amends to the gay community for the loss of lives. There is no mechanism to request forgiveness and clear the mistakes of that time period.

The question then and now as AIDS cases in the young have increased: if they are lovers with someone who is HIV-positive, how much do they need to practice "safer sex"? Most gay men know they must use condoms, even if their present partner tests negative, until the relationship moves to long-term. Traditional men who have had few sexual encounters due to attempting to live a heterosexual life often resist becoming involved with HIV-positive men.

Working with a man who is anxious to develop healthy sexual practices after years of married life meant helping him admit hooking up at the local park or rest stop is not the way to begin his new life. Denial kept him in a long-term marriage, and he continues to use the same defense by having anonymous sex, sometimes without protection. At the same time, he says he wants to have a meaningful relationship with someone who is not HIV-positive. These times continue to challenge the gay community; although they have survived the days of the "gay plague," questions of safety and values continue to surface.

My practice in Boston primarily consisted of lesbians and their heterosexual friends. I launched my counseling by way of the first Lesbian Psychologies Conference in the country. My workshop topic was Lesbian Intimacy, which attracted couples and individuals who wanted more internal resources to combat homophobia in the culture and their biological families. Regulating closeness and distance was the theme of the presentation, and this continued in my private practice. This helped relationships work by combating internalized homophobia as well as by understanding the intensity of woman-to-woman bonding: needing to stay close to combat the culture's lens of sickness and yet moving away from single focus. Clinicians labeled the closeness of same-sex relationships as "merger." My thesis is the balance between closeness and distance is possible even with outside prejudices against lesbian and gay people. Often their families have rejected them, and they are dependent on others for support. Counseling is a good idea, both individually and in a group, in addition to reaching out and connecting with the LGBT community. Eventually, they will face the reality of permanent rejection or seize opportunities for their family members to make amends. Working to ameliorate feelings of guilt and shame imposed on them by the culture gives gay and lesbian people the chance to forgive injustices suffered at the hands of their families.

These are happy days in the gay and lesbian community with the elimination of state and federal legislation prohibiting gay marriage. The buzz about marriage consumes conversations. After four years of legal maneuvering, the Case Against 8 was settled when the California Supreme Court ruled against Proposition 8, which had declared marriage was legal only between a man and woman. In the HBO documentary *The Case Against 8*, two couples courageously make their plea for the right to marry. The portrayal has a powerful personal tone and does not focus on the numerous legal rights marriage contracts allow. This was done deliberately to help the court understand how the inequality of the law profoundly affects the personal lives of people.

When Proposition 8 was struck down, the court made amends to the thousands who had already married and whose marriages had been rescinded after Prop 8 passed.

In addition, the court asked for forgiveness for the years of suffering for those who have lived under the threat of exposure.

Today we celebrate the Supreme Court ruling that the states must now eliminate laws making it illegal for gay and lesbian people to marry. Its findings concluded that it is a discriminatory practice to disallow gay marriage.

Murder in a Small Town

As I write this, it has been seventeen years since the murder of Matthew Shepard in Wyoming. The sacrifice of this twenty-one-year-old gay man—who was tortured and left hanging on a fence—has transformed society's awareness of the hatred and violence perpetrated against gay, lesbian, and transgender people. Matthew's mother continues to diligently work toward enacting anti-gun legislation as a way of contributing to society in honor of her young son. Her pain in the wake of her son's abhorrent murder is unfathomable. Judy Shepard seeks amends from society by calling for an end to gun violence.

We live with the daily reminder of society's mistakes. The newspaper offers constant proof we are often on the wrong path. The media fixates on instances of violence, both nationally and internationally, and we fall victim to this fixation. We need to be mindfully cautious about what we can take in and understand how this affects our outlook on life. It conjures up existential dilemmas as we strive to maintain spiritual balance. The spirit of goodness and love dwells within us and can show us the way each day, fending off negativism. Reaching out to friends and those who benefit from our being on this earth makes a difference.

Questions to Think About

1. How willing are you to make amends to those you have offended?

2. When you feel guilty, do you make an action plan to address the issue?

3. What is your attitude toward those who have lost children to the child welfare system?

4. What is your practice for addressing concern for conflict in the world?

5. How do you introduce joy into your life?

6. Multiculturalism is now our way of life. How do you feel about this?

7. In what ways do you revere Mother Earth?

8. What challenges have you faced in our family?

9. How do you personally address issues of discrimination?

10. Do you make it a practice to include diversity in your life?

Someday, men and women will rise, they will reach the mountain peak, they will meet big and strong and free, ready to receive, to partake, and to bask in the golden rays of love.

—EMMA GOLDMAN, *Marriage and Love*

Chapter VI

Communication/Perception

YOU KNOW WHAT it's like—you swear you saw something, and someone disagrees. They saw it differently. Of course they did, because perception is always colored by what someone wants to see or even by physical barriers to a view. The trick is to let go of being "right" while not changing what you believe based on someone else's experience. How do we make both people right? Acknowledging that we view our world through a prejudicial lens may help. Partners fight over what is real for each person and seek agreement or admission to being the correct one.

In couples counseling, it can be fun to help couples uncover the differences in perception and communication. I often begin the work with an exercise in which I ask each person to talk for under a minute. I then ask the partner to repeat back exactly what was said, literally, using the same words the partner spoke. I ask the second person to do the same. Invariably, we discover one person is more literal and the other is interpretive. One hears almost the exact words while the partner is more abstract—analyzing what is being said, reading into the message, or looking for a motive behind the message. Next, I encourage the couple to help each other stay with the literal message, speaking more clearly.

The rules of communication can be simple, but a willingness to practice the principles is necessary for changing old patterns that do not work. Speaking for ourselves, avoiding generalizations, and working toward eliminating guilt-tripping and blame are a few helpful tips. Often one partner will make statements about what the other believes or what they are thinking. The problem with reading our partner's mind is that what was once true may no longer be the case. People evolve over time, so the things that used to be true may no longer be so. Change in one person is challenging for the partner, who needs time to adjust.

Vera has decided to take up running. As the mother of two preschoolers, she requires planning and cooperation from her partner. Daycare makes it possible for Vera to become a strong runner. This new passion also means time away from her partner and children in the evenings. Dan, her partner, resents that Vera has chosen to be on her own without him. She puts terrific energy into running, understanding she also likes the time away from Dan. Discussions of her love for the sport are tense and sometimes unfruitful. At times, Vera was tempted to give it up to placate Dan as he whined from the sidelines. There was no happy solution to this dilemma because Vera went on to develop friendships with other runners, entered races, and spent considerable time away from the family. She admittedly saw running as a time out from the relationship. In counseling, the couple was able to be more honest about their feelings, and agreements were made to ensure they made time for dates, had daily check-ins via text and email, and arranged in advance for daycare to facilitate both of their schedules. First, however, they needed to decide whether they wanted to remain in the relationship and commit to whatever it took to make it work.

Jimmy and Marla came in with similar communication issues. Jimmy assumed because he was establishing a company that his responsibility for household duties was out of the question. Marla was willing to take charge of the house, but she had no homemaking skills. Things were complicated by the fact that they were raising special-needs twins. The news that their boys were injured struck both of them hard. She got busy arranging for the programs and home care required, and this served as a helpful defense against despair. Jimmy got busier outside the home and became an alcoholic. This couple demanded serious sorting out, and I had reservations about how to proceed. Obviously, the drinking had to be addressed, which meant an almost complete turnaround in his job habits. I also helped him acknowledge the disappointment of having children who were not perfect. He was driven by perfectionism and needed to understand the injury to his children was not his fault. Much speculation could be made about who did what during the pregnancy, but this is not helpful in getting to what needs to change in the moment. Honest communication between them meant recognizing how each blames the other for the twins' situation.

How do we communicate honestly about such painful situations? When a child is afflicted, the parents tend to consciously or unconsciously blame the other for the problem. Sometimes injury can be traced to the origin, but then what? Is forgiveness the appropriate way to go, or is acceptance more important? If honest communication can be established but blame persists, individual counseling is needed to work through the resentment and find a clearing, a way to live without the underlying resentment.

If Jimmy wants to continue his lifestyle and Marla wants to change but stay in the relationship, she needs to reach beyond Jimmy for comfort and satisfaction. When my own daughter was diagnosed as brain-injured, I looked outside my family to find not only myself but what I loved to do. Art became a wonderful outlet and being active in the Civil Rights movement helped me grow. Communication with my husband deteriorated, and we divorced. Toward the end, I said that for me to consider staying in the marriage, my partner would have to stop drinking. He told me that was impossible. I recall feeling relieved he was the one being asked to stop and not me. I knew I didn't want to be in that position. I was not drinking alcoholically, but booze was fundamental to my way of life. My perception was that if people just drank casually the way I did, things would be fine. This is a prevalent attitude among partners when alcohol is interfering with the relationship.

Dialogue

A COMMON AXIOM is that matters of politics and religion should not be discussed when there are profound differences between parties. Dialogue, however, can generate agreements, and it is possible to engage in discussion while respecting each other's beliefs. The democratic process is supposed to foster consensus among congressional members. At present, there is a severe schism between parties, and this intensifies the polemics. If we believe there is no way to resolve conflicts, however, we will cease to participate in elections and in our own personal lives, for that matter.

Gut reactions are guides that force us to pay attention to our feelings. This can be hard when you are trying to figure out what is going on with someone you love. For years, I tried to get in touch with myself while being challenged by my alcoholic son. When I look back, I realize I was up against terrific defenses—my own and my son's. There were times when he was overtly manipulative, slick, and self-seeking. I suspect he felt guilty for setting me up for failure. No matter what I did, there was no way he was going to give up alcohol. The cycle was obvious: get drunk, become a different person, find trouble, hurt people, land in jail, lose the driver's license—all while desperately trying to keep a job. It hurts to be saying these things now that he is gone. I had tried so many approaches, including time out for months at a time. Nothing worked. Eventually, I was able to communicate boundaries: no drinking when with me and no hangover behavior when we saw each other. These rules were difficult for Tom, but he managed pretty well, and we had some good experiences together. Today, I continue to pay attention to my feelings as the grief can become overwhelming. I try to keep the pain of loss at bay; it comes anyway, but at least I have taken my life back. Plus, I no longer have the constant worry about the health and well-being of my son.

Anger Management

IT CAN BE frustrating when another person just doesn't "get it," no matter what we do. If it's a coworker or neighbor, this can be managed by avoiding contact as much as possible.

In couple relationships, agreements are important. I ask couples to limit their conflictive discussions to an hour or less, abiding by the rules of communication as much as possible. When things become unmanageable, a time out can cool things off. Someone has to call for time out, citing when they will be back. Asking for "space" is a worn-out phrase and overused. The other party may not be ready; this is why agreed-upon standards are a must. Saying when he or she will be back offers hope for the person waiting. Being left hanging can be painful.

Time out is the first rule of thumb when managing anger. When I listen to couples describe their conflicts, tone often determines what the other is experiencing. One describes the other as yelling when it is just the passion of the moment and voices are not really being raised. Negotiating tone can be an easy task with the understanding that a stern tone is not raising one's voice or screaming.

Paying attention to our breathing and counting to five before we respond are helpful ways of coping, as is asking our partner to repeat back what they are saying or stating back what you hear. This takes time and can slow the pitch of emotions. Or how about breaking out in a dance or a favorite song? Sounds bizarre, but this requires letting go of the win-lose dynamic of the moment. Exploring what brought people together in the first place also helps.

Juanita had a child at nineteen and was convinced to give her up for adoption. Now, thirty-five years later, her husband, Jerry, is asking her to tell their two adult children they have a sister. Juanita had been waiting for over thirty years for her daughter to seek her out. It never happened. Jerry was anxiously awaiting Juanita's decision to find her daughter, Susan. He felt guilty because he had already found Susan, who had recently died in an automobile accident. Jerry and I met alone, and he disclosed what he had done. This placed me in a dilemma in that now I shared a secret with him, and Juanita was outside the triangle. This is not an unusual circumstance but one therapists should try to avoid. The task was to convince Jerry to disclose what he had done. I found it puzzling that he still wanted Juanita to track Susan down, knowing she was deceased. He offered no rationale to me. As couples counseling proceeded, however, he was not forthcoming to Juanita. He and I met alone again, and I informed him that I would not continue couples work until he told his wife the truth, and he was to inform her of the discontinuance. This placed him in a paradoxical dilemma. He had to disclose the reason for the dissolution of counseling, which meant he had to tell what he had discovered about Susan. He had created a no-win situation for himself. When Juanita called and asked why we weren't meeting, I deferred to Jerry. I am no longer in touch with his couple, and I have no idea how it played out between them.

Play Time and Diversity

A STAY IN Provincetown has always been a wonderful summer refuge for me. The tip of Cape Cod is known as a gay Mecca as well as an artists' colony. So many writers and painters have spoken of the light at the end of this piece of heaven. Recently vacationing there during "Family Week," we discovered the theme was love, encouraging equality for all family formations. It was striking how the town had been transformed during this week, making one aware of why marriage equality is essential. Hundreds of lesbian and gay families attended this special week, comfortably commingling with hundreds of heterosexual families. It reinforced that bigotry cannot be sustained. Observing male couples joyfully pushing baby carts with children of color and coupled lesbians wholly engaged in parenting—including all the carts, bags, blankets, baby toys, and other paraphernalia—stirred many feelings. I missed the "gayness" of this vibrant town but appreciated the longing gay and lesbian couples have for acceptance in their pursuit of family.

Love over Time

LONGEVITY DOES NOT define the quality of a relationship. It is difficult to accept that things change over time and there is no way to make time stop, to maintain the status quo. The realization that changes are happening can be scary. A seasoned relationship is revered in all cultures, but so many people grew up with parents who should have given up this ideal. Resistance to marrying is not unusual in single men and women. Women have children without partners. Recreating misery is not appealing, and today's families often comprise clusters of community-raising individuals.

Sexuality changes over time, and the comfort of familiarity takes its place. It is sad that couples often stop having sex, but it is up to the individuals to make this determination. It does not mean something is inherently wrong with the relationship. I've worked with women who resisted the introduction of Viagra. They say they finally felt a hiatus from the pressure of waiting it out while their partners faced compromised erections. With Viagra, they were expected to enjoy sex again, when these women actually felt relieved they did not have to perform.

When lesbians stop having sex, it is attributed to "erotophobia," but there's an acceptance of this transition in lesbian culture. Older lesbians joke about this. Women still have access to sex and orgasm that doesn't involve a partner, even though touching themselves may not have been encouraged.

At sixty-two, Tilly was wooed by a younger woman, Lil, and was flattered to the point that she ended her relationship with her seventy-one-year-old partner, Bonnie. For Lil, midlife had resurrected a longing for nurturance and love for her mother. Instead of working through this issue in therapy, Lil impulsively ensnared Tilly. The ensuing heartbreak was painful to witness. Tilly and Bonnie had been partnered for over twenty years, and the break-up took a toll on them both. Tilly was left penniless when Bonnie died. Tilly had revived her sexual prowess with Lil but ended up harshly judging herself.

As people age, relationships undergo developmental changes, and the hope is that they will ultimately land in a healthy place, with enough shared interests and affection to sustain to the end. It is sad to see older couples split, knowing the despair of loss is debilitating.

Historically, women have stayed in unsatisfying relationships for economic reasons. Those married to wealthy partners found outlets to fill the gap left by disconnection. This financial comfort has often paid off, despite the grief of not feeling revered in their relationships. They report having found alternative sources of happiness as they pursue education, sports, and hobbies.

Busy, Busy

A WONDERFUL WAY to deflect the stress of daily challenges is observing nature and the ways in which birdies and animal life survive. The messages of nature help us settle down inside. Observing animals tracking food every moment of the day may help us be grateful for our lives. Finding ourselves through bonding with nature requires looking at mortality, which can be harrowing, but watching a song sparrow belt out a song while huddled in the pine tree next to you can be thrilling. It keeps us in the moment and deepens our respect for the most vulnerable.

Mothers and Daughters

COMMUNICATION ISSUES BETWEEN mothers and their daughters is a common theme in counseling settings. One woman, Eleanor, discussed an elder sister's death prior to her birth. Her mother hoped she would be a boy, and this disappointment pervaded the household as she grew up. She recounted episodes of physical abuse such as being whipped with a belt to the point of bleeding and being shut away in a room as punishment. The client internalized the rejection of the mother and struggled with a lack of self-confidence. Differentiating herself from how her mother viewed her took years of therapeutic work. Messages of self-doubt had to be countered with affirmations in counseling, group settings, and her relationships. Her attempts at marriage and disconnection behaviors led to suicidal gestures and constant messages of how she could end her life. She suffered from depression, and medication helped over time.

In our Mothers and Daughters classes, we acknowledge that the mother is our first love, and the daughter closely watches and mimics the mother's face. The daughter reflects a face of anger and disappointment. The reorganization of the affect seems a formidable task. Looking at the abuse and releasing the charge it has over the daughter is the counseling work. Eleanor was able to write about her experiences and uncover hidden messages from her mother. So focused on the abuse, she had been unable to retrieve positive attitudes toward her as well as the ways in which her mother taught her an appreciation for art, classical music, and sewing. Now in midlife, Eleanor has these gifts today. As she reviews how her mother was in midlife, Eleanor acknowledges her mother's strengths as well as her weaknesses. Fortunately, her father compensated for her mother's abuse and often told her she was lovable and important to him. Eleanor eventually stopped seeing herself as her mother did and in time started seeking partners more like her father.

Fathers and Daughters

"WHAT IS THE message of the father?" was the central question in our Fathers and Daughters classes. Was the message direct or indirect? If there was disconnection, at what developmental stage did this occur? The job of the father is to love the daughter, unconditionally for the most part, and to serve as a liaison to the outside world, a link to the working world. Mothers play this role also, but at ages ten, fifteen, and nineteen, a daughter may find her father key to transitioning to adulthood. Many variables interrupt this process in our imperfect world, but we hope there is a positive male role model in a daughter's life before she chooses a life partner. Daughters talk about not having fathers, expressing anger at the abandonment of the absent father. The mother can help the daughter idealize the father if he has died or left the family. In our classes, we reviewed photos to look for ways fathers communicated in the family, observing whom he touched physically and emotionally. In my book, *Lamenting Lost Fathers: Adult Daughters Search for the Message of the Father*, women share their stories. The underlying theme is women really *do* want fathers; they want to know about him, about his early life, and his life both in and away from the family. The women speak of the impact their fathers had on their lives, good and bad. Today, as we enjoy the diversification of family life—with roles shared among heterosexual, lesbian, gay, and transgender individuals—balancing the emotional needs that have traditionally been organized around gender will be fascinating to study over time. No matter what gender assignments, we rely on diverse strengths in partners as they share parenting.

In her book *Living Beautifully*, Pema Chödrön talks about the terror of hopelessness and develops a theme of staying connected and learning ways of addressing this fear. Depressed daughters can find relief by practicing new ways of thinking and processing feelings.

Transgender

The New Yorker recently featured a critique of radical-feminist versus liberal-inclusion attitudes toward female-affirmed transgender individuals. Specifically, the piece explored the practice of only permitting women born women into events as well as the formation of groups protesting the lack of recognition of transgender and transsexual persons. Traditionally, the Michigan Women's Music Festival has disallowed those not born women. No resolution has been reached after years of fighting over this issue. It comes down to a disagreement about rights, with one group feeling anyone has the right to address gender privilege and change their gender identification while the other group believes in the right of women to have their own space and define who will join them. Brutality and discrimination follows trans wherever they go, and many think it is sad that some radical feminists refuse to share certain political and social events with female-affirmed trans. The Michigan festival grounds are privately owned, and the owner makes the deliberation as to whether to include trans. Some issues cannot be settled by either/or ideologies. Like in their private living rooms, I feel people ought to be able to decide who will be invited onto their property without triggering harsh feelings of exclusion.

The baggage of gender restrictions needs to be shed in whatever ways possible, and the transgender community often does this. Some fear trans individuals are seeking change because they want erotic connection with the opposite of their birth gender. Young people are trying on trans for size, seeking sex with trans and figuring out what is best for them. In all relationships, experimentation is part of sexual development. So if being trans includes sexual eroticizing, why should we care? If it is not our path, we can be helpful to others who are figuring out what they want. I love the phrase, "It's not the end of the world," and maybe this is the time to take that attitude, especially as we implement medical systems that serve every population.

Questions to Think About

1. Do you acknowledge differences in perception when communicating?

2. Are you willing to practice principles of good communication?

3. Do you nurture friendships outside your primary partnership?

4. Do you want to practice honest communication?

5. Are you willing to dialogue with those who do not share your political or religious beliefs?

6. What is a standard rule of thumb for managing conflict?

7. What is your understanding of developmental changes?

8. How have rigid gender definitions impaired social progress?

9. What is the message, direct and indirect, of your father?

10. Do you acknowledge the gifts or talents passed on to you by your mother?

*I love and dance with my dream unfurled,
trusting darkness, trusting the labyrinth, into
the furnaces of love.*

—ANAÏS NIN, *Cities of the Interiors*

Chapter VII

Check to See How You're Doing Every Day

MUCH HAS BEEN written about God, and it seems every author/teacher has a different name for this Supreme Being. It's fascinating to peruse the literature, noting the terms being used to convince followers of ways to either join God or be God. Thinking of ourselves as God can be appealing. Internalizing a being that helps us navigate through the day's challenges is a powerful practice. In AA, we are warned about ego and the results of "me" thinking. I find the term, "just another Bozo on the bus" helpful in combating ego's fateful path to drinking or festering resentments. That being said, each of us has to figure out a way not to give into self-defeating thoughts and actions.

A simple mantra such as "blah, blah" might chase away messy thoughts. We don't have to believe we are special to effectively clear our mind. Offering ourselves to someone, anything, more powerful than us works if we can really give in and let go of control, even if it's just for an hour. I remember a client who suffered anxiety and commandeered order in all aspects of her life. We had great chats that I'm not sure led anywhere, but one tactic helped her identify when she was being controlling and perfectionistic: I asked her to keep a crooked painting hanging in her living room. It drove her nuts at first, but later she found it helpful in tracking her state of mind based on her urge to straighten the picture versus when she could care less about it.

One of the early readings on meditation suggests lighting a candle, staring at it for a minute or so, then closing our eyes and still seeing the lit candle. This is relaxing and helpful, and when I work with people who are attempting elaborate meditations and are critical of themselves for not "doing it right," I make the above suggestion to help them simplify their practice. It seems like a contradiction to impose rigid standards of meditation, even with the caveat that we should do the best we can. Avoiding useless guilt and shame is critical to healing. Meditation is a wonderful combatant to stress and its effects on the nervous and immune systems. It calms the limbic area of the brain, which monitors emotions. Meditating for two minutes just twice a day is a good way to manage the pull of worry and anxiety.

I scanned a book on the basic principles of Buddhism and quickly bumped into a focus on death and backed off. Maybe I am guilty of pushing away from death, and it is true I am weary of the subject, but I want to help people live better lives *now*, without the idea that death is at every door and with less looking forward to a life in the hereafter. Harboring thoughts of the end of life before it's time to prepare seems a waste. There is much to live for if, indeed, we have only one life. Erik Erikson's theory on generativity is inspiring: by way of example, we can pass on to others what we have learned. I believe this has more merit than obsessing about life beyond.

Embracing Change

MY LATEST AWAKENING is that we really can embrace change. This means looking at our environment, paying attention to new buildings, and looking at the use of the land—even something like constructing condos in the middle of town—without grumbling. Hanging onto the notion that we will always have our own private view of a nearby mountain or just the right distance from a neighbor may not be realistic or possible. People have always lived on top of each other in our culture. Letting go also applies to people. Clinging to past friendships as people die or grieving distant relatives who have moved on with their own lives may not serve us as we face each day. We need to find new "tricks" to help us stay in the day, to welcome change. If we don't agree with the change, one option is protesting online through social networks or with organized groups. Believing these systems will actually effect change is a brave attitude, and it takes courage to work on behalf of our convictions.

A recent documentary features an elderly man walking the state of Utah and another older gentleman who takes teams of people on trips through the Utah wilderness. Both of these men were willing to try new things to keep them moving—literally. Not all of us can physically take on such endeavors, but we can design our own ways to take risks, try new things, and use our bodies in ways that strengthen us physically and mentally.

A young man I knew briefly took to mountain climbing because this was his first love: to be outdoors alone in beautiful surroundings such as Arizona and Colorado. He died in an accidental fall down a mountain, but everyone who knew him reconciled his loss with the fact that he died doing what he loved. It was apparent that he focused on life rather than obsessing about death. Sometimes his kind of risk-taking can be a prelude to suicide, without the gestures or intent. Many of his friends felt his carelessness spoke to his inability to become physically limited. Finding compassion for those he left behind and avoiding judgment can still allow for the anger his family feels.

Compassion

COMPASSION FOR OURSELVES cancels shame and regret. When I make a blunder, I try to deal with the triggered feelings. I understand they go back to the meanness with which I treated my mother as a young child, so I make sure I figure out a way to either make amends or take some kind of action that will help ease my guilt. It is compassion for that little girl who was trying to survive that pulls me through the residual feelings. This is the same compassion and empathy I express with my clients. It touches the same spot in my psyche and enables me to be helpful. With trainees, I stress that our life experiences are often a guide when working with others. Objectivity has its place, but understanding someone else often requires having "been there."

Every day when I returned from school, I knew my mother would be "resting," as she called it. She was weary from her outing partly due to her age, but she intuitively knew sleep was crucial to continuing her day. Recent studies are verifying that sleep is essential for physical and brain health. No less than seven or eight hours is the recommendation. For some, this may mean retiring later rather than going to bed early and complaining they cannot sleep past 4:00 a.m.

SLEEP is fundamental. If you have trouble sleeping, practice changing thoughts, say a mantra, listen to relaxing audiobooks, pet your cat, or talk to your dog. Sometimes reading can help get you back to sleep.

For restlessness, **COOK** something. Concentrating on a recipe builds intellectual strength and helps with tracking as you prepare for the puzzle. Both hemispheres of the brain are working at the same time. Feeding the stomach feeds the soul, and researching recipes online enhances your internal search engine.

My friend sits with the sunrise every morning. This quiets her thoughts and places her in awe of her place in the world as a small dot living just for that day. She says it reduces her grandiosity. She knows she is an overachiever who has difficulty constraining herself and holding back her opinions. The rising sun reminds her she is not the center of the universe but also encourages her to do her best without pressure to be in control. She asks, "Who controls the sun?" Something in the universe is bigger than her.

WALK it off. Every morning after chores and breakfast, I begin my day with a walk. This is my way of recalibrating my brain, which often betrays me in the early hours. It helps to be walking somewhere, so I target my course to include reading the newspaper or writing. Maybe it means meeting a friend for coffee or lunch. This helps develop community: connecting with people walking their dogs or talking on their phones; keeping track of who's moving in, who's moving out; or chatting with neighbors while strolling by. We can also listen to informational presentations, good music, or news of the day on an iPod or other device.

If you are a water person, **SWIMMING** builds the body and takes us back to the womb. Rivers and lakes are perfect in the summer, and an inside pool at the YMCA or motel sustains the practice of immersing our bodies into a weightless environment. A freezing cold dip in a river or the ocean awakens every nerve and skin surface, clearing the mind.

The Women's Center

THE COMPELLING TITLE Women in Transition brought hundreds of women together to make changes in their lives. This was the 1970s, when women were escaping the kitchen and returning to school and work, and they knew they needed support to address the resistance they experienced from their husbands, children, and family members. Sitting in a circle exposing their fears, frustrations, and anger about the oppression they felt was liberating. Much has been written about this time in herstory, and it was powerful to be at the center of a momentum that would change American women's experience forever. While the abortion debate rages on today, we were witnessing women taking control over their bodies, relationships, and futures for the first time. This was after the birth control pill had been introduced and the first layer of oppression lifted. It was time to help women listen to their honest inner voices, feelings, and opinions. Out of these group meetings came strategic actions to work for change in political and social settings. It involved a tremendous amount of education: designing courses; impacting traditional coursework; and teaching social service agencies how to work differently with women, children, and eventually men. Out of a simple workshop on household violence came a whole movement about exposing domestic and sexual violence in relationships and families.

Today if you observe a local bulletin board, you will see flyers about groups addressing personal development and change. While the feminist movement was working for change in women's lives, the Human Potential Movement was conducting seminars and retreats to help alleviate the confusion and oppression of traditional thinking. When I was an anti-racism trainer in Detroit, principles of freedom and the history of struggle in other countries were part of our trainings. Group work is irreplaceable in that consciousness-raising occurs quickly, and people stretch themselves to make personal and social changes.

Every time we turn on the television and witness a group like those protesting racism or classism, we are thankful the push for real change lives on. So, **GROUP WORK** is a good way to make a difference in our own lives as well as effecting change in the larger culture.

Recently, I was diagnosed with a form of skin cancer (basal cell carcinoma) on my face. This required elaborate surgery and other procedures on areas of concern. While I was always grateful my baldness was not due to cancer, I was aware skin cancer was possible, given that sun worship was the norm in my era. Now, as the cancer group walks are forming, I will join in to acknowledge the seriousness of this disease. Cancer is the issue of our age, and it's important to join the struggle for increasing research and services. Over the years, I have worked with several cancer survivors and witnessed their reactions to medications. I tried to be helpful in their decision-making and walk with them through their sadness and fear. Each client learned how to value the day, not think too far into the future, and stay hopeful. These are lessons for all of us as we learn how to stay present and avoid worrying about the future.

When my children were little, I realized I needed something just for myself that would keep me grounded in my parenting. I began to **PAINT**. I placed my easel in the path of the backyard where neighborhood children tended to play with my children. My son would pass by and exclaim, "Mom, that's pretty!" Or he would say, "That looks funny." He had a good eye at an early age and was a great critic. When I decided to paint, I went to the art store and bought a set of oils and canvas. I just started—without lessons or worrying I was doing it wrong. I have always practiced artistic endeavors just because it worked for me, not because I wanted to sell or show my stuff.

That came later. So I make a big case for being self-taught, just like I had to be growing up with elderly parents of a large family. I am grateful they were as burnt-out as they were because they weren't overly critical of me. I think we can be our worst critics, and as soon as those negative feelings come up, I dash them away with the realization that I am having fun. Fun first, serious later. Finding the painter in yourself is thrilling, especially when you leave the critic outside in the cold.

Each day brings a new possibility to try new things and keep moving. Keep moving in whatever ways you can, pushing whatever limits you need to do this. Reach out for help to figure it out. When I'm with my daughter Molly, I watch her challenge herself just to walk, and she reaches out for help. When she's in a wheelchair, it makes me aware how lucky we are that she can do what she can to participate in her life.

During that awakening time between sleep and awareness, distorted thinking can set in. A quick mantra can pull you through to the beginning of the day. Decide what you will do first, get up, and start there. If we make a list on paper and post it where we can see it, that decreases the pressure, especially if we can check off each item as we go. This is a mindful way to care for ourselves. This sounds like simple logic, but in reality many people have not been shown obvious ways to address responsibility and self-care.

TAKE ACTION. When it came time for Molly to leave our house at age twenty and move into a group home with her peers, there was no such program. Molly's teacher, a friend from County Mental Health, and I wrote a grant to start the first group home for "profoundly mentally retarded" individuals. After we got the grant, setting up the board and finding a local home fell on me. This was accomplished within a year, and prior to Molly's graduation from high school special education, she became the first resident in our group home. We headed upstate to Fairview Institution and chose nine more clients to live with Molly. I always felt I was in the nick of time when it came to acquiring services for Molly as she was often one of the first in need of complex services. Today, there are three houses and one respite under the umbrella of the Ashland Supportive Housing (ASH) program in our town.

WRITE it out. Write your thoughts and feelings. For some, this means journaling daily if possible. Write to take a look at yourself, write not for others but for YOU. Much of our writing evolves into a poem or short story we may wish to enter into a contest. You can also attend a workshop on writing about your life. This idea never becomes outdated because each one of us has a unique story. A writers group allows you to speak aloud what is on your mind, share what you created out of one word you heard that day, or talk about what you read that sparked a whole passage. This means having a good **COMPUTER** and a tech contact who can answer your questions and help problem solve when you get stuck. If money is an issue, the local library has computers and printers for public use.

Maybe it is time to get a good **CAMERA** and wander about shooting photos of whatever comes your way. In time, you will develop your own genre, your favorite images of the seasons, birds, trees, fences, a dewdrop, or your cat or dog in that special pose. Clients of mine who are genuinely wonderful photographers share their pictures with me. It is during this time that we are able to delve into what they were feeling when they shot that special photo. Sometimes it is the tiniest aspect of a scene; they go deeper, seeking a more profound meaning in the object or detail of nature and exploring what it represents to them.

MAKE A GRATITUDE LIST. For years, my good friend has made a gratitude list each day. He often writes it out during his AA meeting. This habit serves as his calming mechanism, helping him get through the repetition of the meeting and keeping him grounded. It is his treatment for anxiety to stave off his tendency to worry about the future.

I recently read of a nearby town burned to the ground by out-of-control fires in the bordering forest. My mood had been edgy, tired of routine, feeling impatient with the work that lay ahead of me that day. Wow, I quickly changed my tune. I looked around my home and thanked it for being steadfast, so lovely, reflecting my and my partner's way of life. My gratitude list changed the tenor of my day. It is easy to forget how fortunate we are to be alive another day. This realization should be more prevalent when we consider the level of slaughter occurring in the Middle East, Africa, and elsewhere. But somehow we are able to separate ourselves from these atrocities and relax in a coffee shop, take a stroll, or go shopping.

SURPRISES happen everyday. The phone rang and *voilà*, the voice on the line was a thirty-year-old son who had been adopted at birth. Now forty-eight, the birth mother, Toni, was married with four adult children and five grandchildren. He called her "Mom," and she was confused and upset. He expressed joy at having found his "family," and he had great expectations of her and planned a visit to meet his half-siblings. Her question was, "Am I supposed to love this man whom I do not know; how can I tell him I don't want him to call me or come visit?" These reunions are supposed to bring great joy and resolution. In reality, they often are a dead end after the initial meetings when people discover they have little in common. Sometimes the young girl who resides in the adult woman who was forced to give up her child does not want to revisit the pain of that time in her life. Toni was wise enough to realize the guilt and shame of the past was what she had to face to give her son what he wanted. She decided she was not ready for that trip down memory lane. Glad that her son was able to get answers to his questions, she finally told him that he would have to move on. I reassured her that this decision could be made "just for now."

TRAVEL. Not all of us can afford to travel, but even a short trip can help us get out of our own way. I love that phrase because it truly speaks to the way we feel when we are bored or worn out. Art shows in nearby towns take us into the world of color, of possibilities. You can attend a music festival or enjoy a late night out, absorbing the lives around you.

DANCING. Most people feel they need to take lessons or join a dance class to have fun. The riskiest thing to do is just dance, let your body go where it wants to take you. Again, you are changing the chemistry of the brain, which helps free you from the dreads. You are transformed into the Dread Raven, which will protect you from bad stuff. At least that is the legend. Even without the legend, we can delve into our internal raven, the smartest of birds, one who can solve mysteries and problems.

Learning to **PLAY AN INSTRUMENT** can be challenging but also deeply rewarding once you get the hang of it. I learned to play the guitar, and now I create songs, which means I need to **SING**. I don't have the greatest of voices, but I can figure out the particularities of my own style. I can shout it out like so many artists do with the strum of a chord in the background. I would never have guessed I would sing with my guitar in the park. Inside

I'm thinking, "What the hell, what does it matter?" Life is too short to worry about being judged.

Although it was difficult, I recently had to give up my two favorite foods—bagels and scones—to get to a more healthy weight. It saddened me to give up the rituals that went with eating these delicious treats. Sometimes I cheat, of course, and spread the bagel throughout the day, as if I am fooling my body. Maybe it won't notice I am embellishing. They call these "comfort foods." Studies show, however, that such foods actually create more anxiety because we know we shouldn't be eating them. This may be true, but there may be times when only a cream donut will stunt the agony of starving oneself. So I say figure out the comfort food and indulge every now and then. It solves the problem for the moment, and you can address the guilt later on. This does take a certain amount of discipline, no doubt, but sometimes withholding a favorite food can be a form of self-punishment, which is not good. If you can find a healthy alternative that is also delicious, you can have your cake and eat it, too.

Questions to Think About

1. Do you want to practice new ways to meditate?

2. What is your understanding of generativity?

3. Are you engaged in activities to impact social change?

4. How do your life experiences inform you in working with others?

5. Do you get enough sleep?

6. How do you quiet your thoughts?

7. What physical activities do you do regularly?

8. What are your views regarding personal development?

9. Are you paying attention to eating habits? Can you make changes?

10. What is on your daily gratitude list?

I choose not to suffer uselessly to detect primal pain as it stalks toward me flashing its bleak torch in my eyes.

—ADRIENNE RICH, *The Dream of a Common Language*

CHAPTER VIII

A Conclusion

IS THERE REALLY ever an end to the self-analysis needed to grow and become a better person, capable of managing the pain and harassment that comes into our paths? Probably not, although pausing to observe a full moon or a reflection in a nearby pond comes close to being equally important. This writing has been a form of self-reflection for me, and it is my hope that it has been a worthwhile adventure for you. I hope it inspires you to WRITE your thoughts, feelings, and opinions as a way of reaching beyond the walls of isolation. Taking good care of yourself is a way of showing your love for others who care for you. Staying close to a best friend is both satisfying and helpful. Personal counseling is another form of self-care.

In personal and business relationships, I am impressed at how women are able to combine the two. For me, this is what makes organizational networking relevant. Men have traditionally done this through discussions of sports or business, and women have talked about family, grandchildren, and maybe some business strategy. Meetings with colleagues now involve personal disclosure as well as addressing the political and social conditions of the world. This enables us to follow over time the developments in our lives and express our opinions of how the world is being run.

Sometimes we conclude if women really had shared power, they would run things differently. We have no way of measuring whether this would be true, but our gut feeling is things would be different. It seems like a tall order when we consider the status of women in the world. The image of hundreds of men on their knees praising Allah suggests there will be a long wait before women actually run the world. Not in our lifetime, most likely. Many of us are discouraged by the constant threat of war. When we review the history of the last hundred years, we see how violence played out in the most primitive ways. Some of those practices still prevail, but we have always had to cope with and overcome fear to live daily life. Markets pop up in Iraq, Syria, Afghanistan, and Africa after the bombing ceases. People know they have to sell their wares to survive. We can only imagine the sense of community that develops during those times.

At a recent book and author festival, I served on a mystery discussion panel. Several in the audience were fledgling writers. Afterward, one man told me he was a motorcyclist and was aware of the famed violence of some of the local and national biker organizations. He spoke of the violence against women he had witnessed over the years and expressed guilt because he had not intervened. I told him it was an important story he could consider writing—a story about what it felt like to have done nothing because of fear of his motorcycle club buddies. This was a powerful breakthrough because he spoke about his inability to follow his personal code of ethics. This brings us back to an earlier question: what can we do in the face of such realities?

Social media is a way many are coping. This is great except when it interrupts being present with family or stops us from activities like reading or working on a brain puzzle. What a fabulous time to be living in—finding answers to questions at the tip of our fingers through Google. Our grandmothers would be astonished to go online and witness the news even before it is really the news!

Having children requires **PLAYING** with children. When I was growing up, this was not stressed or even discussed. We found our own way, but it may be different now, depending on the parents' work hours and their resulting fatigue. We see little ones with their own electronic toys, pushing images and figuring out how to follow the theme of the game. Meanwhile, Mom or Dad is playing their own game on the phone or console. It's too soon to assess how this affects family cohesion, but this kind on non-interaction needs to be monitored by the adults. How fun it is to lean in to the child and follow the game together when the parent understands how important connection is.

All of this makes a great case for daycare and early childhood intervention. Right now, I am attempting to work with a family of marijuana and alcohol users. Teasing out the capacity for conflict resolution from how life would be without altering their reality is a formidable task. In many ways, it is too late for this family. If one stops the daily use and tries to change the dynamics, the other members reject her, and the pressure to rejoin the dysfunction can be more compelling than staying clean and sober. This is the time when the sober member must separate herself, but she is financially dependent to the point that she cannot fathom how this can happen. Drug-dependent herself, she must consider enrolling in one of the programs available for mothers with children who want to live in a sober environment. The financial rewards for staying may outweigh the strength it takes to get out of her situation.

As therapists, we wait for the right moment to intervene, but rejection after rejection is discouraging. In the meantime, the baby in the family remains at risk. As the clinician in contact with this family, I am responsible for doing my best, even though the prognosis is dim. This is an opportunity for me to measure my own efficacy and retreat when I am in over my head.

These cases sit in my consciousness like a cloud about to burst into a rainstorm. I never know where the storm will take me, but if I stay humble enough to understand, my clients continue to teach me the best way to work. My life experience informs me about the origins of my strengths and my limitations as a mere human. Remembering both enables me to do my life's work.

When my son died, I thought it might be the worst assault and wondered if I would ever be spared the wretchedness of this level of pain. Each day presents a new challenge, but the intensity has abated for now, over two years later. I am beginning to reflect on the times we shared and the strengths he possessed. Yesterday, I remembered our trips to an Asian-owned restaurant and recalled the ways in which he would draw the staff into discussion about their day. He would tell them how much he enjoyed a certain season or presentation. He displayed respect for their work while I sat back, hesitant to be so forward. But that was his way, and I miss that deeply. He had wonderful social skills and an ability to engage every-one he came into contact with. This was the sober Tom; in time, I was no longer exposed to the alcoholic Tom, so I was fortunate in that way. I have all of those stories tucked away in my consciousness, too, though. More and more, I feel less need to go over those bad times in my mind.

January is the month of two birthdays (mine and my partner Marie's); an anniversary; and now, the marking of a death. Tom is in my thoughts every day. We learn to put the unfathomable into a context of sorts. I recall saying to clients in the past, "Death is a part of life." Now I think what a stupid thing that was to say to someone in unbearable pain. Psychotherapy and counseling often involve teaching what we have learned or believe true.

I don't disclose to many the death of my son. I think it is too much to put out there; it causes too much pain for others. I have enough of my own, and I don't need to impose that on others. When I was able to resume my daily walks a few days after his death, I did go to my neighbors and tell them. I did this because I have chats with this couple whenever I walk, and I felt it important to tell them why I was often unable to compose myself. Since that day, they have been wonderful allies. When Tom was in the hospital dying, I sent out an email telling friends and relatives, mostly because my partner was prompting me to do so. This was followed by the announcement of his death.

There really is nothing that can be said to a mother that "works" when a child dies, but it is impressive that people try to console. "Sorry" will do it, really. People say you will never be the same or that things will never be the same. I'm not fond of this kind of consolation. Everything in me wants things to go back to normal, and there are moments when they do. The task is to "normalize" the loss of someone you gave birth to and to dash away the memories as they intrude. Put them away until you are ready to look back in a comforting or humorous way, maybe laughing at the irony, the knowing somehow that this was the way things would turn out. My life has had challenges and hurdles, some of which were laid at my feet and others I created for myself. Eventually, I will get there, being able to remember without the stab of pain or rage that this is the way it is.

Life teaches us many lessons, and this has been one of them for me. I now have the ability to reach in and access an agony my clients bring when they experience the absence or loss of someone they love or when they must face illnesses in themselves or in those they cherish.

In reviewing these chapters, my thoughts turn to those who cannot practice these suggestions for changing our thinking and examining buried feelings. There are reasons for this. I would be dreaming to think this writing would be a great help to those engaged in the struggle to simply survive. The challenge of putting food on the table in the absence of resources can be all-consuming. Those living on the street suffer physical limitations, emotional stress, and exposure to people who live by selling drugs or themselves. My wish is that someone, somewhere, will be in a position to **HELP** and share resources.

I hope the words in this book will leave the page and lift your consciousness in a lasting way and that you will benefit in whatever way is best for you.

References

Boston Lesbian Psychologies Collective. *Lesbian Psychologies*. University of Illinois Press, Chicago, 1987.

Cameron, Julie. *The Artist's Way: A Spiritual Path to Creativity*. Souvenir Press, Limited, 2012.

Campbell, Joseph. *The Hero's Journey*. Harper & Row, 1990.

Chödrön, Pema. *Living Beautifully*. Shambala Publications, 2012.

Chopra, Deepak. *The Seven Spiritual Laws of Success*. Amber-Allen Publishing, 2010.

Dunn Dalton, Rosemary. *Lamenting Lost Fathers: Adult Daughters Search for the Message of the Father*. iUniverse, Lincoln, NE, 2004.

Erikson, Erik. *Identity and the Life Cycle*. Oyster Books, 1959.

Frankl, Viktor E. *Man's Search for Meaning*. Google Books, 1946.

Gamble, Foster. *Thrive: What on Earth Will It Take?* You Tube, 2013.

Herman, Judith. *Trauma & Recovery*. Basic Books, 1997.

Hoffman, Alice. *The Museum of Extraordinary Things*. Simon & Schuster, New York, 2014.

Jordan, Judith; Walker, Maureen; and Hartling, Linda. *The Complexity of Connection*. Guilford Press, New York, 2004.

Kramer, Larry. *The Normal Heart*. Plume, 1985.

Lee, Jackie. *Make Way for Winged Eros: A Book of Days*. Pomegranate Books, Rohnert Park, CA, 1963.

Maslow, Abraham. Psychology Paper. 1943.

Nestle, Joan; Howell, Clare; and Wilchins, Riki. *Genderqueer: Voices from Beyond the Sexual Binary.* Alyson Books, New York, 2002.

Perry, John. *The Art of Procrastination: A Guide to Effective Dawdling, Lollygaggling, and Postponing.* Workman Publishing, 2012.

Rich, Adrienne. *The Dream of a Common Language: Poems 1974–1977.* Penguin Books, Markham, Ontario, 1978.

The Nature Conservancy. nature.org/oregon.

Hạnh, Thích Nhât. *Anger: Wisdom for Cooling the Flame.* Deckle Edge, 2002.

Rosemary Dunn Dalton LCSW

ROSEMARY DUNN DALTON is a licensed clinical
social worker in private practice and a former adjunct
faculty member of the Southern Oregon University
Psychology Department. Dunn Dalton was awarded the
SOU Distinguished Alumni Award in 2006. Featured in
Feminists Who Changed America, 1963–1975, she coedited
Lesbian Psychologies and authored *Lamenting Lost Fathers:
Adult Daughters Search for the Message of the Father*. Dunn
Dalton also writes mystery novels, including *Arches Trea-
sure & Mystery at the Escalantes; Bandon-Vernal Transgender
Mystery & The Jacksonville-Donner Story*; and *Lost and Found*,
a poetry chapbook. Dunn Dalton enjoys painting, playing
guitar, writing plays, and spending time with her partner,
Marie, and her two daughters, Molly and Brigid.

www.ingramcontent.com/pod-product-compliance
Lightning Source LLC
Chambersburg PA
CBHW051813040426
42446CB00007B/647